23|6|06

Promoting the health of
older people

RETHINKING AGEING SERIES

Series editor: Brian Gearing
                 School of Health and Social Welfare
                 The Open University

'Open University Press' *Rethinking Ageing* series has yet to put a foot wrong and its latest additions are well up to standard . . . The series is fast becoming an essential part of the canon. If I ever win the lottery, I shall treat myself to the full set in hardback . . .'

Nursing Times

Current and forthcoming titles:
Miriam Bernard: **Promoting health in old age**
Simon Biggs *et al.*: **Elder abuse in perspective**
Ken Blakemore and Margaret Boneham: **Age, race and ethnicity**
Julia Bond and Lynne Corner: **Quality of life and older people**
Joanna Bornat (ed.): **Reminiscence reviewed**
Bill Bytheway: **Ageism**
Anthony Chiva and David Stears (eds): **Promoting the health of older people**
Maureen Crane: **Understanding older homeless people**
Merryn Gott: **Sexuality, sexual health and ageing**
Mike Hepworth: **Stories of ageing**
Frances Heywood *et al.*: **Housing and home in later life**
Beverley Hughes: **Older people and community care**
Tom Kitwood: **Dementia reconsidered**
Eric Midwinter: **Pensioned off**
Sheila Peace *et al.*: **Re-evaluating residential care**
Thomas Scharf *et al.*: **Ageing in rural Europe**
Moyra Sidell: **Health in old age**
Robert Slater: **The psychology of growing old**
John A. Vincent: **Politics, power and old age**
Alan Walker and Tony Maltby: **Ageing Europe**
Alan Walker and Gerhard Naegele (eds): **The politics of old age in Europe**

Promoting the health of older people
The next step in health generation

Edited by
ANTHONY CHIVA
and
DAVID STEARS

OPEN UNIVERSITY PRESS
Buckingham · Philadelphia

Open University Press
Celtic Court
22 Ballmoor
Buckingham
MK18 1XW

email: enquiries@openup.co.uk
world wide web: www.openup.co.uk

and
325 Chestnut Street
Philadelphia, PA 19106, USA

First Published 2001

A catalogue record of this book is available from the British Library

ISBN 0 335 20438 4 (pb)   0 335 20439 2 (hb)

Library of Congress Cataloging-in-Publication Data

Promoting the health of older people: the next step in health generation/edited by
Anthony Chiva and David Stears.
    p. cm — (Rethinking ageing series)
  Includes bibliographical references and index.
  ISBN 0-335-20438-4 (pbk.) — ISBN 0-335-20439-2 (hardback)
    1. Aged—Health and hygiene.   2. Health promotion.   3. Preventative health
services for the aged.   4. Preventive health services.   I. Chiva, Anthony,
1949– II. Stears, David, 1945– III. Series.

RA564.8.P756 2001
613'.0438—dc21

                                                                00-050137

Typeset by Type Study, Scarborough
Printed in Great Britain by St Edmundsbury Press, Bury St Edmunds, Suffolk

To our teachers and mentors

Contents

Notes on contributors

ALISON ALLEN is currently a public health nurse working with older people as a health promotion specialist. She undertook the research into fall prevention with a general practice in the East Kent Health Authority.

SARA ARBER is Professor and Head of the Department of Sociology at the University of Surrey. She is well known nationally and internationally for her work on gender and class inequalities in health and on ageing and gender. She is co-author of *Health Related Behaviour and Attitudes of Older People* and the *Influence of Social Support and Social Capital on Health* (both with Helen Cooper and Jay Ginn, 1999) and *The Myth of Generational Conflict: Family and State in Ageing Societies* (with Claudine Attias-Donfut, 1999). She is currently working on studies of health promotion among older people from minority ethnic groups, how material disadvantage relates to physical activity, and the relationships between social capital and health.

MIMA CATTAN is a manager in Newcastle and North Tyneside Health Promotion Department with a special remit for older people, and a research fellow in the Newcastle University Medical School. Nationally, she is the Chair of the Special Interest Group: Health Promotion, Older People, and has acted as an advisor on exercise and falls prevention. Her publications include papers on the prevention of social isolation and loneliness, accident prevention guidelines and an HEA resource guide on older smokers. Mima is currently working on a PhD on effective health promotion interventions targeting social isolation and loneliness among older people.

ANTHONY CHIVA has worked in education, in secondary schools and later as district health promotion officer. He has worked in the field of education and health, focusing on gerontology as Coordinator of the Centre for Health and Retirement Education, Birkbeck College. Most recently, jointly with the

University of Surrey and the Pre-Retirement Association of Great Britain and Northern Ireland, as Head of Education and Training he has developed masters modules in health promotion. He is also course director of the MSc in life planning.

STEPHEN CLIFT is Professor of Health Education in the Centre for Health Education and Research, Canterbury Christ Church University College. He has research interests in the field of travel and health and is co-editor of *Health and the International Tourist* (1996), *Tourism and Health: Risks, Research and Responses* (1997) and *Tourism and Sex: Culture, Commerce and Coercion.*

HELEN COOPER is undertaking research and a PhD in the Department of Sociology, University of Surrey, and is working with Sara Arber on research projects funded by the Health Education Authority. This research uses secondary analysis to examine age, gender and ethnic inequalities in health associated with socio-economic disadvantage, social capital and social support. A forthcoming report is entitled, 'Ethnicity, health and health behaviour: a study of older age groups'.

MARY DAVIES is a physiologist who works in education and training, including university lecturing for the Aid to Sexual and Personal Relationships of People with a Disability and the British Association for Services to the Elderly. She is currently the director of the Pre-Retirement Association of Great Britain and Northern Ireland, and is particularly interested in life planning and citizenship throughout the life course.

JAY GINN is a research fellow in the Sociology Department of Surrey University and co-director of the Centre for Research on Gender and Ageing. She co-authored *Researching Older People Needs and Health Promotion Issues* (1997), *Health Related Behaviour and Attitudes of Older People* and the *Influence of Social Support and Social Capital on Health* (both with Helen Cooper and Sara Arber, 1999). She has published widely on gender differences in the economic resources of older people and with Sara Arber co-authored *Gender and Later Life* (1991) and co-edited *Connecting Gender and Ageing* (1995). She is currently co-editing a book, *Women, Work and Pensions International Issues and Prospects*, and researching gender, class and ethnic differences in pension entitlements.

GILLIAN GRANVILLE is the Head of Research and Policy at The Beth Johnson Foundation, a national charitable organization, based in North Staffordshire, which aims to develop and research innovative practice development that raises the status and value of older people. She trained as a nurse and health visitor, and worked in primary care settings as a generic health visitor and practice teacher. Gillian has gained her doctorate in researching the meaning of menopause to midlife women. Her other research interests include feminist methodology and the development of a feminist analysis in gerontology. She has published work on health promotion and gerontological nursing, and, more recently, on intergenerational activity as a means of influencing social policy.

PATRICIA HAYMAN has 25 years of nursing experience, of which 15 years have been particularly focused on the caring of the dying in oncology nursing.

Currently, she is working in private counselling practice, including voluntary work as a bereavement counsellor with a local hospice.

NERYS JAMES has 20 years of experience teaching and working in various secondary schools, including deputy headship, and 12 years of advisory and consultancy work with Surrey Education Authority. Her present role as County Consultant for Continuing Professional Development includes responsibility for the induction of newly qualified teachers, appraisal, staff development issues and working with teachers on aspects of classroom practice. Her specialisms are classroom observation and helping teachers to analyse their own practice. She has helped to develop mentoring approaches in Surrey schools. She is a Cruse counsellor, supervisor and trainer.

MATTHEW MORRISSEY is Senior Lecturer in Mental Health in the Department of Nursing, Canterbury Christ Church University College. His interests in the nursing field include sexuality and sexual health, and spiritual dimensions of care of elderly people. His most recent publications include *Sexuality and Healthcare* (1998) and *Alzheimer's: Beyond the Medical Model* (1999).

CAROLINE NASH holds a master's degree in community medicine and a doctorate in health education. Since 1987 she has specialized in research and training in the area of older people's health and empowerment, with the aim of promoting their welfare. She also has a keen interest in alternative health care. Among her recent publications is *Consider the Alternatives: Health Strategies for Later Life* (1998). For the past 15 years she has practised as a registered homeopath and is also a feng shui consultant and reiki master.

ANNE SQUIRE is the Director of Health Promotion at the University of Wales, Bangor and a UWB teaching fellow. She teaches the principles and practice of health promotion to a wide variety of students, including doctors, nurses, social workers, carers and professionals allied to medicine, lay and older people. Anne is particularly interested in empowerment of the disadvantaged and works as a consultant with BASE and HelpAge International, with whom she has worked in Romania.

DAVID STEARS has worked for 32 years in all sections of education: primary, secondary, further and higher education. He is Reader in Health Education and Head of the Centre for Health Education and Research at Canterbury Christ Church University College. His current duties include research, undergraduate and postgraduate teaching in health promotion and health education. He is director of a World Health Organization Collaboration Centre.

KEITH TONES has worked in secondary school teaching and lectured in teacher training, specializing in the psychology of education and educational methodology. In 1972 he established, at Leeds Polytechnic, the first postgraduate course in the UK for health education specialists. He has acted in a consultative capacity for a number of national bodies, including the Health Education Council, Cancer Research Campaign, British Heart Foundation and Alcohol Education and Research Council, and internationally, including the World Health Organization, Pan American Organization, European Commission and various universities in Europe, Scandinavia and Australia. He has published widely and is co-author of the popular text *Effectiveness and Efficiency of Health Education*, and has just published a chapter on health education and health promotion in the latest edition of the *Oxford Textbook of Public Health*. He is also the editor of the international journal *Health Education Research*.

JOANNA WALKER has had an interest in older people throughout her career, commencing as an information officer at Age Concern England on matters of health services and health policy, and continuing at the Health Education Authority in the Education and Training Division. She joined the PRA's newly formed Educational Development Group in the mid-1980s, specializing in educational resources. As a member of the University of Surrey's School of Educational Studies (joint appointment with PRA), she has a developed an academic interest in the changing relationship between retirement, ageing and learning in later life. She published in 1992 with PRA/Age Concern a practical book for personnel managers, and in 1996 a more academic text, *Changing Concepts of Retirement: Educational Implications*. She is a founder member of the Association for Education and Ageing, and edits reviews for its international journal.

BOB WYCHERLEY has worked as a clinical psychologist in a health authority. During this time he developed an interest in empowering and enabling people. This led to his editing and writing a practical group manual on life skills development. Currently, because of his interest in architecture, he is a full-time design student.

Series editor's preface

Now that in the second year of the new century we are some 16 books into the 'Rethinking Ageing' series, it seems appropriate to review our original aims. The series was planned in the early 1990s, following the rapid growth in ageing populations in Britain and other countries that led to a dramatic increase in academic and professional interest in gerontology. In the 1970s and 80s there had been a steady increase in the publication of research studies which attempted to define and describe the characteristics and needs of older people. There were also a small number of theoretical attempts to reconceptualize the meaning of old age and to explore new ways in which we could think about ageing. By the 1990s, however, there was a palpable gap between what was known about ageing by gerontologists and the very limited amount of information which was readily available and accessible to the growing number of people with a professional or personal interest in old age. The 'Rethinking Ageing' series was conceived as a response to that 'knowledge gap'.

The first book to be published in the new series was *Age, Race and Ethnicity* by Ken Blakemore and Margaret Boneham. In the series editor's preface we stated that the main aim of the 'Rethinking Ageing' series was to bridge the knowledge gap with books which would focus on a topic of current concern or interest in ageing (ageism, elder abuse, health in later life, dementia, etc.). Accordingly, each book would address two fundamental questions: What is known about this topic? And what are the policy and practice implications of this knowledge? We wanted authors to provide a readable and stimulating review of current knowledge, but also to *rethink* their subject area by developing their own ideas in the light of their particular research and experience. We also believed it was essential that the books should be both scholarly *and* written in clear, non-technical, language that would appeal equally to a broad range of students, academics and professionals with a common interest in ageing and age care.

The books published so far in the series have ranged broadly in subject matter – from ageism to reminiscence to community care to pensions to residential care. We have been very pleased that the response from individual readers and reviewers has been extremely positive towards almost all of the titles. The success of the series appears therefore to justify its original aims. But how different is the national situation in gerontology more than ten years on? And do we now need to adopt a different approach?

The most striking change is that, today, age and ageing are prominent topics in media and government policy debates. This reflects a greater awareness in the media and among politicians of the demographic situation – by 2007 there will be more people over pensionable age than there will be children.[1] Paradoxically, however, the number of social gerontology courses is actually decreasing.[2] Why this is so is not entirely clear, but it is probably related to the difficulties which today's worker-students face in securing the time and funding to attend courses. Alongside this is the pressure on course providers to respond only to the short-term training needs of care staff through short, problem-focused modules. Only a few gerontology courses are based around an in-depth and truly integrated curriculum, one that draws upon the very many different academic disciplines and professional perspectives which contribute to our knowledge and understanding of ageing.

There appears to be even more interest in ageing and old age than when we started the 'Rethinking Ageing' series, and this persuades us that there is likely to be a continuing need for the serious, but accessible, topic-based books in ageing that it has offered. The uncertainties about the future of gerontological education reinforce this view. However, having now addressed many of the established, mainstream topics, we feel it is time to extend its subject-matter to include 'emerging topics in ageing' and those whose importance have yet to be widely appreciated. Among the first books to reflect this policy were Maureen Crane's *Understanding Older Homeless People* and John Vincent's *Politics, Power and Old Age*. Most recently, Mike Hepworth's *Stories of Ageing* was the first book by an author based in the UK to explore the potential of literary fiction as a gerontological resource. *Promoting the Health of Older People* is another welcome addition to the 'Rethinking Ageing' series. It reflects the increasingly significant contribution which health promotion is making to the knowledge and understanding of the health and well-being of older people. In future, we hope to continue to rethink ageing by revisiting topics already dealt with (via second editions of existing titles) and by finding new titles which can extend the subject matter of the series.

Brian Gearing
School of Health and Social Welfare
The Open University

References

1 *Guardian* (1999), 29 May.
2 Bernard, M. *et al.* (1999), in *Generations Review*, 9(3): September.

Foreword

—— KEITH TONES ——————————————

With the ancient is wisdom; and in length of days understanding.

Job 12:12

One in five people in Western society today are over 65 years old; in 2025, one in three of the population will attain that age. There are today, in Britain, 20 times as many centenarians as there were in 1951. There are currently four people of working age for every pensioner; by the year 2040, there will be only two.

There can be few people who are not at least beginning to acknowledge that we are living in societies which are growing inexorably older. Even the young who have, traditionally, been able to defer the unpalatable thought of growing old are now forced to recognize this reality when they are warned by government that they will not be able to rely on state support in their old age. They are regularly exhorted to subscribe to privately funded pensions, since the proportionately few people of working age will not be too happy to contribute to the tax burden needed to provide a reasonable standard of living for the clamouring horde of older people! Add to this gloomy prospect the already negative image of ageing prevalent in Western countries and we who are approaching our twilight years would seem to face a bleak prospect – not least of which are the fiscal and economic strategies that chancellors of the exchequer will be pursuing in order to limit the economic burden about to be imposed by the elderly on the working population. This present book is, thus, particularly timely – especially as it should mitigate some of the gloom and despondency that tends to be associated with the 'problem' posed by the anticipated demands of a large population of older people.

A problem-centred approach is itself problematic – especially the adoption of a traditional preventive medical model which relies overheavily on cost–benefit analysis. It is well recognized that geriatric medicine is expensive: as people get older they typically make substantial demands on health and social services (hence the note of panic and urgency in promoting private pensions and forecasts of subsistence level state pensions). Moreover, even if the curve charting the decline in health of an elderly population can be 'squared', i.e. if the various aches, pains, illnesses and various kinds of distress – to which we will all inevitably be subject sooner or later – can be deferred until relatively late in life, the demand for care and health services will still be there. Accordingly, it is not entirely flippant to observe that the only really efficient cost–benefit strategy is to ensure that people stay fit and healthy until the point at which they die!

Clearly there are in fact many potential problems requiring a preventive approach – problems, for example, such as the 3,000 people aged 65 years and over who die from falls in the UK each year. It would be, therefore, foolish not to anticipate these and, following John Webster's dictum, 'seek wisely to prevent' them. More important is the fact that although years are indeed being added to life, many of these years are not healthy years. According to the current British government's health policy, *Saving Lives: Our Healthier Nation*, at present men's average life expectancy is some 75 years, and, on average, this will include 15 years of longstanding illness or disability. Similarly, of women's 80 years of expected life, 17 years will be spent with some degree of ill-health. In short, we must strive not *only* to 'add years to life' but also to 'add life to years' and 'health to life'.

We should, of course, be wary of considering older people as a homogeneous group. First, by no means are all older people infirm and incapacitated and it is sensible to differentiate between the young, active old and those older people who are genuinely frail and need a good deal of care. To some extent the young old have 'never had it so good' – to borrow Harold Macmillan's classic Panglossian dictum – unless, of course, they are poor. A much more important differentiation, therefore, is to distinguish those who have a reasonable income from those who are eking out a living on state benefits. Inequality and inequity afflict older people just as they afflict society at large. In the recent government inquiry into inequalities in health, it is noted that the mortality rate in people aged 60–74 who had been living in local authority rented accommodation showed a 16 per cent excess, whereas those living in owner occupied accommodation showed a 13–14 per cent deficit. Not surprisingly, life expectancy at age 65 years is 2.5 years greater in men (and two years in women) from social classes I and II than in those men from classes IV and V. Older people from lower socio-economic groups also experience greater morbidity – for example, higher rates of total tooth loss, lower respiratory function and higher blood pressure. To some extent, then, problems of health in old age are merely a reflection of problems at an earlier age: health promotion for older people must therefore begin at a much earlier stage in life.

However, although we must acknowledge the specific illnesses and diseases to which older people are prey, it is both more ethical and more efficient to develop a positive approach and seek to enhance well-being of older people. The most useful way of encapsulating such an approach is in terms of empowerment.

Individual or self empowerment is now generally recognized as a state involving the possession of a relatively high degree of control over one's life and health. Associated with it is a set of optimistic beliefs about life and capabilities and a relatively high level of self-esteem. The 'sense of coherence' popularized by Antonovsky is related to such a desirable state. A sense of coherence involves a belief that life is, in general, manageable, understandable and meaningful – both intellectually and emotionally. A sense of coherence is in most respects healthy and health promoting. There are several studies demonstrating the positive effects of acquiring a sense of control and a belief that life is manageable. For instance, classic studies by Langer and fellow researchers described the health status of a group of frail elderly in a nursing home (who almost by definition had a relatively low degree of actual control in their lives). These older people were encouraged to take advantage of their existing options, such as choosing their own menus. They were additionally invited to have the furniture arranged in their rooms just as they wanted it and were given plants to look after. Not only did they subsequently achieve a higher score on the scale of well-being than a control group, they also lived twice as long.

I mentioned above that a sense of coherence is *in most respects* health promoting. We need to add a caveat, however, about the concept of meaningfulness. Now it is undoubtedly true that individuals with a terminal illness, or people who are living in circumstances that cannot be changed, will be more contented and mentally more healthy if they can ascribe meaning to what is happening to them – for example, being comforted by a strong religious conviction. On the other hand, there is always a danger that a sense of meaningfulness, a feeling that (to quote Voltaire) all is for the best in the best of possible worlds, can be illusory and can stifle initiative. Indeed, in accordance with Marxist notions of 'false consciousness', the existence of such a level of unfounded optimism has been a device for maintaining flagrant injustice and inequity for centuries. In other words, perhaps the most important aspect of empowerment is the possession of that mix of critical awareness, indignation and a conviction that it is really possible to change things. Together with the skills needed to do so, this will lead to social action and social change. It is well recognized that as a result of the socialization occurring in most Western societies, older people are likely to have negative attitudes to ageing, together with low expectations and a feeling of helplessness. Accordingly, the single most useful strategy for promoting the health of older people is one that seeks to empower individuals and, above all, to mobilize the community of older people. The contemporary interest in 'social capital' is clearly relevant to this assertion. Equally if not more relevant is the Ottawa Charter for Health Promotion's major goal of fostering the achievement of an 'active participating community'. While the frail old may make a relatively small contribution to active campaigning, the vigorous young old could quite readily be mobilized. Although the prospect of an active chapter of 'Hell's Grannies' might seem somewhat comical, an organization of 'Grey Panthers' in the USA has in fact undertaken such a role. There are many issues about which older activists and their allies might organize. In fact, the current English government's drive for a 'healthier nation' has explicitly talked about 'building a better Britain for older people', and its proposed aims look beyond the traditional preventive approach to older people. They include: *healthy living* (a principal aim for the new Health Action Zones is the health problems of older people); *income* (acknowledges the problem facing those on moderate incomes); *employment* (acknowledges the expertise and experience of older people and calls for a more flexible approach to retirement); *travel* (acknowledges the health-related implications of transport policy for older people); *at home* (stresses the importance of a warm and comfortable home); *tackling crime* (acknowledges the all-round damaging effect on mental and social health of crime and anti-social behaviour in the community); *care and carers* (recognizes that many of the six million carers are themselves pensioners – and need support); *active lives* (argues for the importance of helping older people to stay active and continue with life-long learning).

As with all health promotion, a broad *horizontal programme* (which deals with the underlying social, economic and environmental determinants of health) rather than *vertical programmes* (that concentrate narrowly on diseases or disease-related behaviours) is more likely to achieve efficient results not only for the promotion of well-being and positive health but also for the prevention of disease. However, radical action costs money – and the attainment of a really effective 'healthy public policy' that addresses the fundamental causes of ill-health in older people will only happen if there is sufficient public pressure to persuade government to invest money and if necessary actually increase taxation. There is, however, a potentially dramatic source of political pressure readily available. I noted above the dramatic increase in the number of older people; if older people were to use their votes and the power resulting from their numbers, they could form political pressure groups having considerable clout. Clearly, the young old who are showing an increasing and welcome tendency to be assertive would need to take the lead; they would also need the support of a coalition of health promoters and health workers. Examples already exist of community-wide coalitions that have launched initiatives which have achieved quite substantial progress. For instance, 'The Boise Experience' – a programme designed to 'build a positive image of ageing' in a small American city – created an effective coalition which ultimately appears to have produced a sea change in older people's attitudes, capabilities and health. In short, they were empowered both as individuals and as a community. During the first 30 months of the programme, some 3500 older adults (approximately 20 per cent of the population of 60 and over) participated in the scheme – and this resulted in measurable effects on their health and well-being. Their average age was 70. Apart from the behavioural and health outcomes generated by the coalition, important changes in local policy directly ascribed to the programme were recorded. Moreover, the initiative had a general 'knock-on' effect on policy at the state level. Aspects of the programme were also replicated in 30 other states nationwide and, at a national level, the programme was recognized by a US Department of Health and Human Services Award of Excellence.

I have so far, in this foreword, argued the case for adopting a radical and horizontal approach to health promotion for older people. Needless to say, if we are serious about getting to the roots of health problems, we should also adopt a lifespan approach and consider ageing from a health career perspective. After all, the factors that create inequality and inequities in the health of the whole population – whether they be children or working age adults – also lay the foundations for inequity in the older generation. To try to address such issues for people once they have achieved the age of 65 is to take action far too late. Similarly, the negative attitudes to ageing in general and to specific life events such as retirement are laid down quite early in people's health career. Health education and health promotion for ageing starts in youth.

Readers might note that this book was written in the United Nations International Year of Older Persons. The UN has identified four central issues, all having implications for horizontal programmes. They are:

- the situation of older people;
- life-long individual development;
- multigenerational relationships;
- the relationship between population ageing and development.

The programme emphasizes such empowerment goals as *independence, participation, care, self-fulfilment* and *dignity*. As so, by way of emphasizing the importance of this book, I complete my reflections with the words of the UN Secretary General Kofi Annan.

A society for all ages is one that does not caricature older persons as patients and pensioners. Instead, it sees them as both agents and beneficiaries of development. It honours traditional elders in their leadership and consultative roles in communities throughout the world. And it seeks a balance between supporting dependency and investing in lifelong development . . . A society for all ages is multigenerational . . . it is age inclusive . . . and committed to creating an enabling environment for health life-styles as people age.

Acknowledgements

This book has been 'a long time in coming' in the sense that its origins have been in the development of our understanding and view of appropriate ways to value our elders. In this book the term older person is used, as currently it still appears less pejorative by association.

Our specific thanks go to the chapter authors, who have brought their experiences, ideas, and practice to their contributions. We would also like to thank those people who have read scripts or drafts and passed comment on the developing materials: Charles and Anthea Cleary, Patricia Hayman, Terry Larter, Caroline Nash, Joanne Parker and Karen Walker.

We are grateful to the Department of Health for permission to use the Health Survey for England data and to the ESRC Data Archive and Manchester Computing Centre for access to data. The analysis is the responsibility of Ginn, Arber and Cooper alone. The research was funded by the Health Education Authority.

The proem to the next step in health generation

_____ DAVID STEARS AND ANTHONY CHIVA _____

This book attempts to highlight the potential of holistic health promotion in the process of enhancing the positive health status of older people, and also includes some chapters which provide an innovative and fresh approach to negative health prevention among older people.

The task of editing this book has been a challenging and rewarding experience, not least from the standpoint of recognizing the possibilities for promoting positive health. Health promotion is often recognized as a worthwhile activity and investment when directed at young people, 'because they have the whole of their lives before them'. Logically, this argument is associated with an ill-health or disease prevention objective. Health promotion is simply equated with activities aimed at containing or eradicating negative health: for example, the prevention of illness, disease and unwanted states which could have negative effects on a person later in life; to say nothing of the future costs to the health services.

When focusing on older people, however, it is easier to identify the link between health promotion and the objectives of enhancing well-being or positive states of personal experience and fulfilment. Primary health prevention takes a rear seat, while perceptions of health associated with such outcomes as 'quality of life', 'peace of mind', 'emotional security' and eradication of 'dis-ease' are thrust to the forefront. We are therefore directed towards a consideration of positive health objectives when applying health promotion to this age group.

The quest continues for clarification of what positive health, as opposed to the mere absence of disease, really is. Only when a clear understanding is established can a proper relationship be developed between health promoters and the wider public. As epitomized in this book, health is more appropriately viewed as a holistic concept encompassing spiritual, mental, intellectual, social, emotional, physical and sexual well-being. With this concept in mind health promotion is best conducted as a process of informing, equipping and empowering rather than directing and coercing.

Health promotion has been described as being composed of three overlapping spheres of activity: health education; prevention; and health protection (Tannahill 1985). Within this model both health education and prevention are seen as legitimate health promotion activities. Within the context of this book it is useful to distinguish between activities which work towards preventing ill-health, disease, disability and unwanted states, and those that promote positive health and contribute to well-being. However, clearly there are contributions to both aspects of prevention and positive health promotion within the chapters which follow.

Mima Cattan's chapter on practical health promotion is a fitting first chapter, as it poses the question 'what have we learnt so far?' Mima Cattan highlights the lack of strategic planning and investment in health promotion for older people. Although the author makes reference to specific targeted health promotion campaigns that have been focused on older people, it is a revelation that there has been no comprehensive survey mounted of health promotion and older people in the UK. The chapter specifically focuses on the type of health promotion provided by health professionals in the UK. Health promotion specialists are shown to be mainly concerned with accident prevention and other government targeted areas of ill-health prevention (though these areas of health promotion can be innovative and holistic in their approach to health promotion, as epitomized in Alison Allen's chapter). Mima Cattan also refers to the potential of primary health care to promote health. Practice nurses working within primary care and with pharmacists are already used to providing opportunistic health promotion advice and would be ideal facilitators of the kind of health information and knowledge that Stephen Clift and Matthew Morrissey refer to in their chapter on travel health and older people (Chapter 11).

The chapters by, respectively, Ginn, Arber and Cooper, and Gillian Granville (Chapters 2 and 3), both provide important perspectives on health promotion for older people within a broader public health context. These inputs relate in particular to practical issues which underpin health development for this age group. They therefore pinpoint key challenges that lie ahead during the new millennium.

In Chapter 2, Jay Ginn, Sara Arber and Helen Cooper reflect upon their research into health-related behaviour among older people. In doing so they clearly indicate inequalities based on age and gender. This chapter is important, in the sense that it outlines an evidence-based health promotion agenda, which is a central component of the UK government's strategic health plan (DoH, 1999). Public health interventions in the future are likely to be based solely on research and development which offers clear evidence of outcomes.

The chapter indicates barriers to healthy lifestyles which are often beyond the older person's control. These barriers are acknowledged as being socially created. Therefore, certain health-related behaviours are examined by the authors in the context of specific socially created circumstances. The health-related behaviours of diet quality and physical activity of older people compared to younger age groups are focused upon. Analysis of data demonstrates that material deprivation and ageing are negatively related to health behaviour, while gender shows a more complex and variable relationship.

Although the authors acknowledge the part health promotion can play in enhancing the health-related behaviour of older people, they are acutely aware of the influence of social disadvantage. The authors therefore highlight the need for strategic measures to face the poverty and improve socio-economic conditions experienced by this section of society. Such positive changes can only be developed through a genuine partnership on the part of health promoters, local and national authorities.

Older people can be placed in what some science fiction writers have referred to as 'a time warp'. Individuals become stranded in the time warp of old age, with an entry gate of senior citizen status and a departure gate of death. In Chapter 3, Gillian Granville makes us rethink the consequences of this form of social stratification. Her chapter provides an interplay between a definition of citizenship and the potential societal-health damaging effect of a time warp or generation gap. This is a relevant and challenging notion for health promotion because it focuses on the principles of participation and empowerment of people and communities.

The chapter draws on evidence to support a claim that active citizenship has been promoted in the United Kingdom through socio-political, health and educational initiatives, all of which are directed at social inclusion, individual and community participation, and empowerment of people to take an active part/role within their communities. In juxtaposition, the author's description of the generation gap that was created during the latter part of the twentieth century, particularly in the USA and UK, is revealing.

The chapter provides a convincing argument based on a case study for developing intergenerational health education and health promotion by bringing together older people from one generation with young people from another. Indeed, this radical or 'upstream' model of health education (Tones and Tilford 1994) not only has the ability to enhance genuine citizenship through broad-based community involvement, but can provide the kind of intergenerational support found in extended families and close-knit communities of a bygone era.

Robert Wycherley develops the theme of personal growth in his contribution on lifeskills (Chapter 4). His review of key models of adult development leads naturally to a description of skills for successful ageing and continued personal growth. This chapter provides a useful bridge between the humanistic perspective of person-centred support during bereavement and loss and a wider discussion of spiritual health. The bridge comes in the form of 'transcendence in older age', what the author describes as the highest level of skills acquisition during the ageing process. This ultimate goal is epitomized by a management of change which includes acceptance of existential challenges and living beyond the physical body. The author separates this stage of development from a spiritual position by suggesting that transcendence is more closely associated with a state of release from the preoccupations of ageing. Although lack of research prevents a clearer definition and understanding of this advanced lifeskill, it is expected that increased longevity will equate with more experience of this level of skill acquisition. Robert

Wycherley, throughout his chapter, emphasizes the potential of older people to experience positive health and adds the transcendental dimension of health to an already established holistic concept.

The dimension of spiritual health requires a detailed exploration for its impact on health and its relevance to health promotion. As our society becomes more diverse the contribution of secular spirituality and non-secular spirituality (religion) to individuals' understanding of themselves, their potency, health and community increase in relevance (Howse 1999). A question is whether there are spiritual components which have the capacity to enhance health, or are they separate meta-physical entities which lead to different constructs of well-being? A health promoter would be advised to assess the way individuals value and utilize spirituality, meaning and purpose in their own lives and the way this impacts on their health. It has also been suggested that health promoters could undertake specific training in this area (Hills and Stears 1995).

This notion of the spiritual self is further developed in a very reflective way by Caroline Nash in Chapter 5. Caroline reviews the concepts of an ageless self within the context of a holistic approach. She explores holism by considering the way people come to identify themselves as being composed of separate parts, which are fragmented and can be competing with each other. When these parts compete negatively imbalance is created, which may lead to ill-health and disease. By reference to various different cultural traditions and approaches to the whole self, Nash builds an image of a human in which ageing can be limitless; where growth and maturation are continuous. This does not deny the realities of physical ageing, but suggests ways in which even these processes can be influenced (Biggs 1999).

The chapter will be challenging for our current ways of thinking. It asks difficult questions to assist the reader in broadening their understanding of the ageless self. Specifically, it challenges commonly held views concerning the greater integration and harmony that Westerners often believe exists in some Eastern cultures. Clearly, dynamic changes are taking place in most cultures and Caroline Nash is seeking to encourage a process which will contribute to the overall well-being of the individual. She extends the concept of wholeness to the individual within a larger group, the concept of the whole being greater than the sum of its parts and the idea that a division of 'labour' is essential to produce an effective operating community.

Health economics is clearly an important discipline underpinning the purpose and direction of health promotion as applied to older people. This fact is drawn upon in Joanna Walker's chapter on health and productive ageing (Chapter 6). She explores the relationship between human productivity and health status, suggesting that health is central to older people's ability and obligation to be recognized as productive. The chapter contrasts and compares the notion of retirement as a non-productive period of people's lives with the post-industrial and postmodernist concept of '*third-age lifestyle*'. The shift that Joanna Walker highlights for older people in retirement is from a traditional *work ethic* to a third-age *busy-ness ethic,* and, more recently, to a third-age *healthy ethic.* The significance of productive ageing for health promotion is to highlight the extrapolation of self-fulfilment among older people towards an appreciation of health literacy and acceptance of the healthy ethic.

The place of fulfilment and health is considered by Mary Davies in Chapter 7. She includes concepts of illness, health prevention and promotion and considers the underlying causes of many of the difficulties older people can experience in achieving a fulfilling sexual role and life. This includes the need for openness and non-judgementalism concerning the rights of older people as sexual beings on the part of a range of professionals.

These rights may also need to be recognized by older people themselves, because of prevalent ageist views and the stereotyping of older people as 'non-sensual and non-sexual beings'. Mary Davies highlights the particular kinds of problems, their origins and potential means for resolution, going into some depth on practical solutions. Overall, this chapter provides valuable insight into the sexual difficulties and traumas some older people may face if various impairments and disabilities occur. The approach is encouraging because of the clear suggestion that most, if not all, sexual difficulties can be overcome by careful thought, attention and caring for oneself or another.

There are fundamental difficulties in personal and societal attitudes which can collude to reduce the potency of an individual. This may particularly apply if the older person is in residential accommodation, where the attitudes and environment can severely limit opportunities for sexual expression and fulfilment. These issues will need careful attention from those involved in caring and supporting older people.

In Chapter 10, Anne Squire develops the theme of applying current health promotion theory to practice. Following an analysis of theories and models of health promotion in the context of working with older people, the author introduces the notion of a health-promoting residential setting. The settings approach to health promotion has been well documented (Baric 1992, 1993) and theoretically modelled with specific institutions in mind (Beattie 1996; Parsons *et al.* 1996). However, this chapter provides an interesting and potentially stimulating alternative to descriptions of the health-promoting school and health-promoting hospital. The health-promoting residential setting for older people offers a truly holistic approach to health development. It enables health professionals to move away from the medical and behaviour change approaches to consider the full implications of creating an environment for older people which might stimulate mental, psychological, societal, spiritual, physical and sexual health.

In Chapter 8, Alison Allen reports a broad based multi-agency fall prevention intervention within a general practice setting. The chapter highlights the value of sound baseline data, in this case on falls among the older population, to establish a prevention programme. This innovative programme recognizes the importance of recording holistic health gain among the study group. Psychological and physiological changes are monitored against those of a control group of patients. The chapter demonstrates the degree to which prevention programmes can reflect successfully on qualitative and quantitative data, empower older people, and incorporate a holistic health concept.

Patricia Hayman and Nerys James (Chapter 9) continue the holistic approach in their focus on bereavement and its management. Central to their approach is the importance of a knowledge and understanding of the bereavement process, the meaning of attachment, the significance of loss and the 'natural process' of grief. Their placement of bereavement within cultural contexts, and as a component of the transition of change, provides meaning to the process of mourning for the health promoter. Similarly, clarification of grief as a psycho-social process informs the task of providing positive health promotion by highlighting the potentially health damaging effect to older people who become entrapped within the process.

The argument for a 'holistic approach' to working with grief and loss takes an interesting twist halfway through the chapter, where the notion of multiple grief is discussed. It is made apparent to the reader that we are reflecting on the loss of a significant other at a time when the bereaved older person is already in the process of experiencing grief through the loss of elements of his or her holistic health. It is at this point that the authors move towards the positive health-promoting role of supporting agents. The Rogerian influence, used to support the argument for working holistically with the bereaved older person, introduces a distinctive humanistic perspective to the enhancement of positive health of older people, one which has been emphasized by latter-day philosophers of health who recognize the significance of human potential and the potential for personal growth (Seedhouse 1986). The chapter reinforces the argument for the development of health promotion processes that inform, equip and empower older people.

Perhaps it is necessary to place Hayman and James's chapter in the context of 'scientific enlightenment'. The experience of death remains a difficult challenge for human comprehension. One of the twentieth century's most prominent philosophers, Hans-Georg Gadamer, relating how knowledge structured by Christianity had been challenged by scientific investigation, made the following observation:

> But if it is true that even if this scientific enlightenment, like that of the ancient world, finds its limit in the ungraspability of death, then it remains true that the horizon of questioning within which thought can approach the enigma of death at all is still circumscribed by doctrines of salvation. For us, this is the doctrine of Christianity in all its diversity of churches and sects. To reflective thinking it must seem as ungraspable as it is illuminating that true overcoming of death cannot lie in anything but the resurrection of the dead. For those who believe, this is the greatest certainty, while for those who do not it remains something ungraspable, but no more ungraspable than death itself.

> (Gadamer 1996: 69)

The final chapter, by Stephen Clift and Matthew Morrissey, extends the negative health and disease prevention approach. Travel-related health issues are reviewed by the authors, with the intention of highlighting potential and realistic health risks for older people. The descriptive epidemiology used in this chapter is supplemented with references to the holistic health of older people when travelling. Travel-related health issues exemplify a range of relatively new areas of public health risk. Without sufficient knowledge of the potential risks to their health, and self and community empowerment to take preventive action, older people will surely remain a vulnerable group within society.

The central tenet of Mima Cattan's first chapter is the development of a strategic framework for an integrated approach to health promotion for older people. This would need to include the recognition that older people are a diverse group and have a wide range of health-related needs. However, such a strategy will need to include markers for effective health promotion and health education. These markers are illuminated within the pages of this book and include theory and practice which support:

- a holistic appreciation of positive health;
- social inclusion through an integrated approach;
- evidence-based interventions;
- development of health-promoting settings.

In summary, this text attempts to go beyond merely describing health promotion as applied to older people. It provides a mosaic of perspectives on health and health promotion which can be used to inform future debate on, and practice in, health promotion for older people.

References

Baric, L. (1992) Promoting health – new approaches and developments, *Journal of the Institute of Health Education*, 30(1): 6–16.

Baric, L. (1993) The settings approach: implications for policy and strategy, *Journal of Institute of Health Education*, 31(1): 17–24.

Beattie, A. (1996) The health promoting school: from idea to action, in A. Scriven and J. Orme (eds) *Health Promotion: Professional Perspectives*. Milton Keynes: The Open University and Macmillan.

Biggs, S. (1999) *The Mature Imagination: Dynamics of Identity in Midlife and Beyond*. Buckingham: Open University Press.

DoH (1999) *Saving Lives: Our Healthier Nation*. London: Department of Health.

Gadamer, H-G. (1996) *The Enigma of Health*. Cambridge: Polity Press.

Hills, F. and Stears, D. F. (1995) Promoting spiritual health, *Journal of Contemporary Health*, 2: 32–4.

Howse, K. (1999) *Religion, Spirituality and Older People*. London: Centre for Policy on Ageing.

Parsons, C., Stears, D. and Thomas, C. (1996) The health promoting school in Europe: conceptualising and evaluating the change, *Health Education Journal*, 55: 311–21.

Seedhouse, D. (1986) *Health: The Foundations for Achievement*. Chichester: Wiley.

Tannahill, A. (1985) What is health promotion?, *Health Education Journal*, 44:167–8.

Tones, K. and Tilford, S. (1994) *Health Education: Effectiveness, Efficiency and Equity*, 2nd edn. London: Chapman and Hall.

PART 1

Principles to practice

The authors in this first part of the book outline the 'starting points' – the backgrounds – and set the scene for health promotional activities with older people.

Mima Cattan reviews the current state of health promotion, types of activities, government thinking and the new 'campaign' structures of healthy action zones. This is followed by a well documented chapter on lifestyles and associated health consequences from Jay Ginn, Helen Cooper and Sara Arber. Relating to this theme is the role of older people as citizens described by Gillian Granville.

These social analyses are followed by a psychological perspective from Bob Wycherley, who encourages the reader to consider a developmental approach leading to transcendent views of health. The next chapter considers integrative approaches to people and their spirituality and holism. Caroline Nash in a very personal way reflects on the nature of holism and how it arises, and explores myths – challenging the reader with her questions.

1

Practical health promotion: what have we learnt so far?

MIMA CATTAN

Introduction

Until a few years ago health promotion and older people received at best a fleeting acknowledgement in pre-retirement courses. Mostly, once people had reached retirement age the view seemed to be that their health was in steady decline and little could be done to maintain or improve their health status. Recently, however, there has been an increased interest in the promotion of well-being among older people, one of the main reasons being an ageing population. It has been estimated that over the period 1991–2031 the total population in the UK will increase by 8 per cent, while those aged 60–74 will increase by 43 per cent, those aged 75–84 by 48 per cent and those aged 85 and over by 138 per cent (Medical Research Council 1994). Several international and national initiatives, such as the United Nation's International Year of the Older Person (Department of Health 1999a; United Nations 1999), the European Commission's various position papers on healthy ageing (Walters 1996; Eurolink Age 1999), the government's white paper *Saving Lives: Our Healthier Nation* (Department of Health 1999b), the government's green paper *Our Healthier Nation* (Department of Health 1998), the Health Education Authority's Older People programme and the Ageing Well programme (Ageing Well 1994) have served to put the promotion of health in older people on the political agenda.

For older people themselves health means a number of different things: being able to lead an active and disability free life for as long as possible; being able to get out and about; having a companion to confide in and access to a social network; being valued as a contributing member of society; being free of disease; and being able to live and act independently. Health is also considered to be dependent on living in a safe environment, with access to transport, financial security, good housing and adequate heating (Action for Health

1996; Coleman *et al.* 1996; Walker and Maltby 1997). Three key behavioural risk factors – smoking, diet and physical activity – are known to have an impact on several diseases, such as cancers, heart disease and respiratory illness, which are often associated with later life (Grimley Evans *et al.* 1992; Kennie 1993; Doll *et al.* 1994; Ebrahim and Kalache 1996; Walters 1996). Social inequalities and deprivation are equally important determinants of health in old age (Townsend and Davidson 1982; Acheson 1998).

The findings from a recent policy review by the Health Education Authority and the Centre for Policy on Ageing (Killoran *et al.* 1997) suggest that there is a strong case for promoting the health of older people, both in terms of the benefits for the health and well-being of older people, and in terms of the wider economic and social benefits to society. Adding to this, there is an increasing body of research evidence, as well as a wealth of local experience and anecdotal evidence, to demonstrate that health promotion interventions can be effective in improving and maintaining the health of older people (Isaksson and Pohjolainen 1994; Cattan and White 1998; Meyrick and Morgan 1998; Drury *et al.* 1999).

Local health promotion and older people

The main health benefits of health promotion for older people are a longer disease- and disability-free life and improved general well-being (Killoran *et al.* 1997). To achieve this, the promotion of older people's health takes place on several different levels, directly as well as indirectly. According to the Ottawa Charter, health promotion is 'the process of enabling people to take control over and improve their health by: building healthy public policy; creating supporting environments; strengthening community action; developing personal skills; reorienting health services'(Walters 1996). In this chapter I focus on the types of activities that take place locally, rather than on national policies which obviously also have a great deal of influence on local strategies.

Using the Ottawa Charter definition of health promotion, local action which has an impact on and promotes older people's health indirectly includes improved housing for older people, improved public transport and maintenance of the built environment. Action where the main aim is to improve and promote the health of older people include activities which target:

- the key behavioural risk factors known to have an impact on major diseases associated with later life;
- causes of disability, dependency, ill-health or death, e.g. accidents;
- causes of mental health problems, e.g. loss, isolation and loneliness.

These activities may include one or more elements of 'indirect action' and take place in different settings: the home, the community and the statutory services. Action to promote and improve older people's health may be planned and developed at a strategic level or implemented at an individual level.

No overarching survey has ever been conducted of health promotion and older people in the UK. However, attempts have been made, for example, through the Health Education Authority's focus on accident prevention and the Active for Life Campaign to establish a project/activity database (Health Education Authority 1998). The database includes action and interventions on all three levels, ranging from strategy development to local exercise classes. The Health Education Board for Scotland also keeps a register of community projects involved in health promotion (Health Education Board for Scotland 1998). A survey in the North of England of health promotion activities aimed at alleviating social isolation and loneliness among older people found that activities ranged from social activities (going on outings, playing cards, bingo), befriending, social support and having meals together, to physical activity (walking groups, tai chi, dancing), information and advice, and the provision of transport (Cattan and White 1998).

An overview of health promotion programmes in North America and Western Europe found that most programmes for older people covered physical exercise, healthy eating, prevention of frailty and injury, smoking cessation, chronic disease management, appropriate medication, healthy nutrition, social empowerment, immunization, holistic well-being and combined self-care and healthy lifestyle (Kalache 1996).

From reports by members of the Special Interest Group on health promotion for older people[1] it would seem that the majority of health promotion specialists with a remit for older people focus on accident prevention and the promotion of physical activity in the community. A smaller number provide education and training on specific health promotion issues relating to old age, older women's health or carers. A small, but increasing, number are investigating ways of promoting health in institutional settings, such as residential care. Health promotion departments are often expected to support national campaigns, such as raising awareness of hypothermia and osteoporosis, or increasing the uptake of breast screening among women aged 50–65. The effectiveness of such involvement remains unclear (Urban *et al.* 1995; Janz *et al.* 1997; Scaf-Klomp *et al.* 1997), although local qualitative studies reveal that older women, in addition to written reminders for mammography, want written materials, information on video and talks to groups (Vaughan 1996).

The large emphasis on accident prevention and the promotion of physical activity among older people is mainly due to government strategy documents – *The Health of the Nation* (Department of Health 1992); *Our Healthier Nation* (Department of Health 1998), the Allied Dunbar National Fitness Survey (Allied Dunbar 1992; Health Education Authority 1995) – which have shown the consequences and implications of accidents among older people (Askham Glucksman *et al.* 1990; Lilley *et al.* 1995; NHS Centre for Reviews and Dissemination 1996; Department of Trade and Industry 1998) and provided convincing evidence of effective exercise interventions to prevent falls (Oakley *et al.* 1995; NHS Centre 1996; Wolf *et al.* 1996). Studies suggest that for an exercise programme to be effective in preventing falls it should be implemented in combination with other interventions, or with those at particular risk of falling, and it needs to be specific for the purpose (Cryer 1999; Skelton 1999). In addition, qualitative and observational studies support anecdotal evidence that insufficient social support is a key barrier to exercise among older people, and that older adults often participate in physical activity for social rather than health reasons (Cousins 1995; Stead *et al.* 1997). Findings from a review recently commissioned by the European Commission suggest that a substantial proportion of published outcome studies on health promotion interventions targeting older people focus on the effect of physical activity, particularly in relation to the prevention of accidental injury.

The Northern Region guidance document for public health and health promotion on accident prevention in older people (Northern Region Accident Prevention 1999) provides an evidence-based framework on how to go about developing effective interventions locally. The guidelines provide guidance on eight topics specifically: exercise and physical activity; road safety; public transport; housing and home safety; primary care; secondary care; independent nursing and residential homes; the role of hip protectors.

Many people, including older people themselves, are unaware of the health benefits for older people from other key lifestyle changes – smoking cessation, improved nutrition and diet, and reducing alcohol consumption – even though the evidence is quite clear (Frierson 1991; Grimley Evans *et al.* 1992; United States Public Health Service 1992; Doll *et al.* 1994, 1997; Fletcher and Rake 1998; Cattan 1999a). Unfortunately, very few published studies are available to demonstrate the effectiveness of specific interventions in these areas. This means that although we know that lifestyle changes can make a difference to older people's health, we do not necessarily know which interventions on smoking, diet or alcohol will have the greatest impact.

The enthusiasm among practitioners, whether primary health care staff or community workers, for interventions targeting lifestyle changes among older people varies greatly. Despite the convincing evidence of the benefits of smoking cessation for older adults, and the demonstrated effectiveness of opportunistic advice by general practitioners (Raw *et al.* 1998, 1999), studies show that smoking is rarely approached by GPs with older people (Bridgewood *et al.* 1996; Cattan 1999a). Older people themselves mostly believe that the damage is already done and that nothing can be done to reverse it (Orleans *et al.* 1994; Bridgewood *et al.* 1996). A number of studies have demonstrated that tailored smoking cessation programmes for older people in primary care and in specialist clinics can be effective (Vetter and Ford 1990; Rimer and Orleans 1994; Hirsch 1996). The first is based on the cycle of change model, which suggests that in order to quit smoking, smokers will advance through five motivational and behavioural stages: pre-contemplation, contemplation, preparation, action and maintenance or relapse (Prochaska and Di Clemente 1983).

Similarly, alcohol and safe drinking are rarely tackled in health promotion and older people. Although studies have shown that alcohol is a contributing factor to depression and suicide, particularly among older men (Dennis and Lindesay 1995; Draper 1995), poor health, such as malnutrition, cancers, gastric problems, liver damage and heart disease (Ward and Goodman 1995; Graham and Schmidt 1998) and accidents (Ashley *et al.* 1997), there are few studies which have investigated the effectiveness of specific interventions relating to drinking behaviour in later life (Fink *et al.* 1996). One study, where a multimedia community education programme provided information and skills regarding alcohol abuse among older people for families, older adults and service providers, found that programme participants had significant gains in knowledge and in intent to take appropriate action in response to alcohol problems (Pratt *et al.* 1992).

The OXCHECK study, which investigated the effectiveness of health checks performed by nurses in primary care in reducing risk factors related to heart disease and cancer, found no significant difference between the intervention group and the control group regarding smoking cessation or alcohol consumption, but a significant effect from dietary change. The researchers concluded that the benefits of health promotion in primary care were clear, but that these had to be weighed against cost benefit (Coulter *et al.* 1995; Imperial Cancer Research Fund 1995).

There is some evidence to suggest that community pharmacists may be effective in providing opportunistic health promotion advice, especially with some training on, for example, behavioural change (Sinclair *et al.* 1997; Raw *et al.* 1999). The advantages of pharmacists are that they are accessible, many older people see them more regularly than anyone else in primary care and they may be more aware of the older person's use of both prescribed drugs and medication bought over the counter.

In contrast to smoking and alcohol interventions, there is a great deal of enthusiasm for nutrition and healthy eating programmes for older people in the community. Old age is seen as a time of increased risk of poor nutrition. Diseases, drugs and alcohol may interfere with uptake of important nutrients, or eating patterns may change as a result of social isolation, depression, dementia or reduced income (Fletcher and Rake 1998). The most recent diet and nutrition survey undertaken in the UK found that people aged 50–64 had lower average energy intakes than adults up to the age of 50. Energy intakes were also lower for those living in households receiving benefits, among unemployed men and for women in lower socio-economic groups (Finch *et al.* 1998). There are probably several reasons for the enthusiasm for nutrition and healthy eating projects in the community. They are seen as an opportunity for older people to get at least one low-cost, nutritious, warm meal per day which they might not otherwise be able to afford or have the energy to prepare. They offer a platform for social interaction and social support. They offer a forum for training, advice and information on food preparation and healthy eating. In the survey of health promotion practice targeting social isolation and loneliness among older people, 26 of 136 projects stated that meals were provided for and/or prepared by older people as part of their aim to alleviate isolation and loneliness (Cattan and White 1998). Several projects included an educational element on food preparation (for widowed men), nutrition and healthy eating on a budget.

An American survey of a large scale programme in the United States, the Elderly Nutrition Program, aimed at highly vulnerable elderly populations, including those near or below the poverty line, people with significant health conditions, minority populations and people living alone, judged the programme to be successful in improving nutritional intake and decreasing social isolation (Ponza *et al.* 1996). As the programme was designed under US legislation to meet specific American needs, some limited lessons may be learnt and transferred to a European environment, such as the benefits of targeting health promotion programmes at specific population groups, and the role of nutrition programmes providing social support.

Unfortunately, there remain major gaps regarding well evaluated nutrition programmes in the European context (Fletcher and Rake 1998). Consequently, practitioners will for some time yet continue to depend on their own experience, anecdotal evidence and evaluation studies from elsewhere.

As was seen in the survey of activities to alleviate social isolation and loneliness, community projects aiming to enhance the well-being of older people employ a wide range of activities and methods to achieve their goal (Cattan and White 1998). These include information and advice on, for example, healthy living and services, and how to access these, the provision of personal skills education and training, and the provision of social support. A two-year follow-up evaluation of the Wallingford Wellness Project, a community-based health promotion programme for independently living older people, revealed a long-term effect on sustaining participant improvements in lifestyle habits (physical fitness, stress management, nutrition) and acquired health information. However, improvements in mental health (decrease in depression), health service utilization and reduced risk of heart attack and stroke, which had been demonstrated at the six month follow-up, were not sustained. The researchers suggest that this may in part be owing to decreased involvement in health promotion classes over the two years, and that continued intermittent programmatic intervention may be required in order to sustain long-term effects of health promotion interventions (Lalonde *et al.* 1988). The Stanford Five-city Project, although not specifically targeting older people, demonstrated that community intervention approaches were effective in lowering the risk of cardiovascular disease (Fortmann *et al.* 1995).

On a national level the Ageing Well programme, managed by Age Concern England, aims to 'promote effective models of healthy ageing' by making use of volunteer senior mentors who are trained to provide information, advice and counselling to their peers (Ageing Well 1994). Process evaluation has been carried out which suggests that the model is a viable way of achieving increased health knowledge and behavioural change (Walters 1996; Woods 1997). Other studies have suggested that trained lay volunteers acquire substantial health gains through their participation in health promotion (Vinokur Kaplan *et al.* 1981; Redburn and Juretich 1989).

The concept of lifelong learning received government backing in 1998 (DfEE 1998). It is known that mental stimulation through education and training has long-term health benefits (Cusack 1995). The aim of the University of the Third Age (U3A), which functions around several hundred local groups, is to encourage lifelong learning for those no longer in full-time gainful employment (Minichiello 1992; U3A 1999).

Establishing an effective Health Promotion Strategy for older people

As has been shown, there are a considerable number of different initiatives, nationally and locally, within a variety of frameworks, which promote the health of older people. Not only can this seem confusing for someone planning a health promotion programme for older people, but it will inevitably lead to activity not being targeted appropriately and scarce resources being wasted unnecessarily. The development of a strategic framework for both current and planned health promotion activity provides an effective tool for a comprehensive and integrated approach to health promotion among older people.

Before setting out to develop a local health promotion strategy for older people we need to bear in mind that older people are a diverse group, in terms of age, health and fitness, dependency, socio-economic status, levels of social exclusion, ethnicity and gender. A strategy, whether an overarching health promotion strategy or one more specific, such as an accident prevention strategy, needs to have this diversity incorporated into targets and action plan.

The Irish Health Promotion Strategy for Older People (Brenner and Shelley 1998) highlights eight special considerations which have strategic implications for health promotion:

- some people enter old age with chronic disease;
- the risks of cancer, heart disease, stroke and respiratory disease are higher in older people;
- the increased tendency towards loss of fitness, mobility and strength with increasing age;
- poorer vision and hearing may contribute to less social contact and increased risk of accidents;
- the association between age and less capacity to recover quickly from illness;
- the change in dietary and nutritional requirements with age;
- the risk of psychological distress as a result of factors associated with ageing, such as loneliness, bereavement, adjusting to retirement, inadequate income, poor health and functional incapacity;
- mental health problems, such as depression or dementia, being a common cause of disability among older people.

Based on the lessons learnt from developing a local accident prevention strategy for older people, the process of producing a successful and viable strategy will include the following elements (Cattan 1996b):

- access to local data relating to health and older people;
- a survey of local health promoting activities for older people;
- time to develop a framework for the strategy, and time to develop and agree an achievable action plan;
- continuous support for multi-agency collaboration (partnerships rarely happen automatically!);
- the development of internal and external networks arising from the strategy working group;
- additional 'spin-offs', e.g. surveys, or the development of projects;
- members gaining as well as contributing to the group;
- older people as equal members of the working group to ensure that the strategy is in touch with reality;
- regular review and update of the strategy and its action plan;

- a couple of 'champions' to ensure that the strategy is endorsed and its implementation supported.

In practice this would mean that older people's needs would be identified and a survey of what is already in place to meet those needs conducted. The time required to develop a strategic framework and a realistic action plan would depend on the level of commitment to the strategy, the effectiveness of joint working and how well older people are able to participate in the process. The Action for Health senior citizens group in Newcastle identified six key barriers to accessing services which equally are barriers to participation:

- cost;
- transport to and from services;
- location;
- attitudes towards older people;
- information;
- physical access.

For effective networks and partnerships to develop the targets would need to be based on evidence of older people's needs, and owned by all. The strategy offers a framework whereby it is possible to work towards the same goals while utilizing different methods. Strong partnerships often generate activities. Voluntary organizations and older people themselves are particularly well placed to identify areas for immediate action in the community: for example, establishing an exercise class or a food co-op. Through the strategy network potential partners, funding and skills can be located. With recent legislative changes in the UK it has become easier to tie health promotion strategies to the wider health goals. Health Improvement Programmes, Health Action Zones, Healthy Living Centres, Primary Care Groups (or Trusts) and Local Health Care Co-operatives (in Scotland) are all potential vehicles for taking forward health promotion in older people.

Once in place, local health promotion strategies need to be sustained. A strategy is never static. It should evolve with emerging evidence to meet changing needs and expectations. The action plan should be reviewed and changed in line with new evidence of effectiveness. Local strategies for the promotion of exercise and physical activity in older people need to take into account the evidence of effectiveness regarding mortality and morbidity as well as regarding the maintenance of exercise behaviour. Continued commitment and successful partnerships at all levels need to be maintained and coordinated to ensure long-term sustainable results. Otherwise there is a risk that organizations or individuals continue to work in isolation, that opportunities are not recognized and consequently lost or that older people's expectations are raised unrealistically.

It goes without saying that any health promotion initiatives and activities intended to improve and maintain the health of older people should be acceptable and accessible to older people themselves. Evidence has demonstrated that health promotion interventions have been effective where older people have been part of the process of developing, implementing and reviewing the intervention. Older people should be recognized as integral to the entire process, and not simply as recipients of well meaning health promotion activities.

Characteristics of an effective health promotion strategy for older people include the following:

- The strategy recognizes that older people are a diverse group regarding age, health and fitness, dependency, socio-economic status, levels of social exclusion, ethnicity and gender.
- The process includes sufficient time to collate baseline data, develop a framework, support partnership working, network development and potential project development, and review the strategy and its action plan.
- Older people are integral to the process of developing, implementing and reviewing the strategy and the associated action plan.
- Targets are based on evidence of older people's needs.
- The strategy is endorsed by all organizations implicated in the action plan, and continued commitment is maintained to ensure long-term, sustainable results.
- The strategy recognizes that different methods can be utilized to achieve common goals.
- Potential vehicles for taking forward the strategy include Health Improvement Programmes, Health Action Zones, Primary Care Groups/Trusts, Local Health Care Co-operatives (Scotland) and Healthy Living Centres.
- The strategy is allowed to evolve as a result of changing evidence, service delivery and needs and expectations of older people.
- Barriers to participation for older people in the development of the strategy are addressed.

Note

1 The Special Interest Group is a network of health promotion specialists with a specific remit for older people. For further information, contact Mima Cattan (Chair), Newcastle and North Tyneside Health Promotion Department, Park View House, Front Street, Newcastle upon Tyne NE7 7TZ, or Age Concern England, Walkden House, 10 Melton Street, London NW1 2EB.

References

Acheson, D. (1998) *Independent Inquiry into Inequalities in Health Report*. London: Stationery Office.

Action for Health, Senior Citizens in Newcastle (1996) *The Links to a Fuller Life*. Newcastle upon Tyne: Healthy City Project.

Ageing Well (1994) *Ageing Well: Health Promotion with Older People*. London: The National Council on Ageing.

Allied Dunbar (1992) *Allied Dunbar National Fitness Survey: A Report on Activity Patterns and Fitness Levels*. London: Sports Council, Health Education Authority.

Ashley, M. J., Ferrence, R., Room, R. *et al.* (1997) Moderate drinking and health – implications of recent evidence, *Canadian Family Physician*, 43: 687–94.

Askham, J., Glucksman, E., Owens, P. *et al.* (1990) *A Review of Falls to Elderly People*. London: DTI.

Brenner, H. and Shelley, E. (1998) *Adding Years to Life and Life to Years. A Health Promotion*

Strategy for Older People. Dublin: National Council on Ageing and Older People, Department of Health and Children.

Bridgewood, A., Malbon, G., Lader, D. and Matheson, J. (1996) *Health in England 1995: What People Know, What People Think, What People Do*. London: OPCS.

Cattan, M. (1999a) *Older Smokers: A Practical Resource for Health Professionals*. London: Health Education Authority.

Cattan, M. (1999b) Accident prevention strategy into action. BGS Spring meeting, Cork, Ireland, unpublished.

Cattan, M. and White, M. (1998) Developing evidence based health promotion for older people: a systematic review and survey of health promotion interventions targeting social isolation and loneliness among older people, *Internet Journal of Health Promotion*. www.monash.edu.au/health/IJHP/1998/13

Coleman, P., Bond, J. and Peace, S. (1996) Ageing in the twentieth century, in J. Bond, P. Coleman and S. Peace (eds) *Ageing in Society: An Introduction to Social Gerontology*. London: Sage.

Coulter, A., Fowler, G., Fuller, A. *et al.* (1995) Effectiveness of health checks conducted by nurses in primary care: final results of the OXCHECK study, *British Medical Journal*, 310: 1099–104.

Cousins, S. O. (1995) Social support for exercise among elderly women in Canada, *Health Promotion International*, 10(4): 273–82.

Cryer, C. (1999) Physical activity, falls and accident prevention – the evidence. Paper presented to Physical Activity and the Prevention and Management of Falls and Accidents conference, Sheffield.

Cusack, S. A. (1995) Developing a lifelong learning program – empowering seniors as leaders in lifelong learning, *Educational Gerontology*, 21(4): 305–20.

Dennis, M. S. and Lindesay, J. (1995) Suicide in the elderly: the United Kingdom perspective, *International Psychogeriatrics*, 7(2): 263–74.

Department for Education and Employment (1998) *The Learning Age: A Renaissance for New Britain*. London: Stationery Office.

Department of Health (1992) *The Health of the Nation*. London: Stationery Office.

Department of Health (1998) *Our Healthier Nation*. London: Stationery Office.

Department of Health (1999a) International Year of Older Persons, *Target, Our Healthier Nation* (32). London: Stationery Office.

Department of Health (1999b) *Saving Lives: Our Healthier Nation*. London: Stationery Office.

Department of Trade and Industry (1998) *Home Accident Surveillance System: 20th Annual Report*. London: DTI.

Doll, R., Darby, S. and Whitely, E. (1997) Trends in mortality from smoking-related diseases, in J. Charlton and M. Murphy (eds) *The Health of Adult Britain 1841–1994*. London: Government Statistical Service.

Doll, R., Peto, R., Wheatley, K., Gray, R. and Sutherland, I. (1994) Mortality in relation to smoking – 40 years' observations on male British doctors, *British Medical Journal*, 309: 901–11.

Draper, B. M. (1995) Prevention of suicide in old-age, *Medical Journal of Australia*, 162(10): 533–4.

Drury, E. (ed.) (1999) *Proven Strategies to Improve Older People's Health*. London: Eurolink Age.

Ebrahim, S. and Kalache, A. (eds) (1996) *Epidemiology in Old Age*. London: BMJ Publications.

Eurolink Age (1999) Secretariat Update, *Eurolink Age*. London: Eurolink Age.

Finch, S., Doyle, W., Lowe, C. *et al.* (1998) *National Diet and Nutrition Survey: People Aged 65 or Over*. London: Stationery Office.

Fink, A., Hays, R. D., Moore, A. A., and Beck, J. C. (1996) Alcohol-related problems in older persons. Determinants, consequences, and screening, *Archives of Internal Medicine*, 156(11): 1150–6.

Fletcher, A. and Rake, C. (1998) *Effectiveness of Interventions to Promote Healthy Eating in Elderly People Living in the Community: A Review*. London: Health Education Authority.

Fortmann, S. P., Flora, J. A., Winkleby, M. A. *et al.* (1995) Community intervention trials – reflections on the Stanford 5-City project experience, *American Journal of Epidemiology*, 142(6): 576–86.

Frierson, R. L. (1991) Suicide attempts by the old and the very old, *Archives of Internal Medicine*, 151(1): 141–4.

Graham, K. and Schmidt, G. (1998) The effects of drinking on health of older adults, *American Journal of Drug and Alcohol Abuse*, 24(3): 465–81.

Grimley Evans, J., Goldacre, M. J., Hodkinson, M., Lamb, S. and Savory, M. (1992) *Health: Abilities and Wellbeing in the Third Age. The Carnegie Inquiry into the Third Age*. Dunfermline: Carnegie United Kingdom Trust.

Health Education Authority (1995) *Health Update 5: Physical Activity*. London: HEA.

Health Education Authority (1998) *Accident Prevention among Older People: A Database on Accident Prevention Initiatives in England*. London: HEA.

Health Education Board for Scotland (1998) Welcome to HEBSWEB/Databases, www.hebs.scot.nhs.uk

Hirsch, A. (1996) Stopping smoking: assessment of methods. *Oncology in Practice*, 1: 6–8.

Imperial Cancer Research Fund (1995) Effectiveness of health checks conducted by nurses in primary care: final results of the OXCHECK study, *British Medical Journal*, 310: 1099–104.

Isaksson, P. E. and Pohjolainen, P. (1994) *Health of the Elderly: A Review of the Effectiveness of Health Education and Health Promotion*. Utrecht: IUHPE.

Janz, N. K., Schottenfeld, D., Doerr, K. M. *et al.* (1997) A two-step intervention to increase mammography among women aged 65 and older, *American Journal of Public Health*, 87(10): 1683–6.

Kalache, A. (1996) Health Promotion, in S. Ebrahim and A. Kalache (eds) *Epidemiology in Old Age*. London: BMJ Publications.

Kennie, D. (1993) *Preventive Care for Older People*. Cambridge: Cambridge University Press.

Killoran, A., Howse, K. and Dalley, G. (eds) (1997) *Promoting the Health of Older People: A Compendium*. London: Health Education Authority.

Lalonde, B., Hooyman, N. and Blumhagen, J. (1988) Long-term outcome effectiveness of a health promotion program for the elderly – the Wallingford Wellness Project, *Journal Of Gerontological Social Work*, 13(1/2): 95–112.

Lilley, J. M., Arie, T. and Chilvers, C. E. D. (1995) Accidents involving older people: a review of the literature, *Age and Ageing*, 24: 346–65.

Medical Research Council (1994) *The Health of UK's Elderly People*. London: MRC.

Meyrick, J. and Morgan, A. (eds) (1998) *Health Promotion Effectiveness Reviews*. London: Health Education Authority.

Minichiello, V. (1992) Meeting the educational needs of an aging population – the Australian experience, *International Review of Education*, 38(4): 403–16.

NHS Centre for Reviews and Dissemination (1996) *Preventing Falls and Subsequent Injury in Older People*. York: University of York.

Northern Region Accident Prevention, Older People Group (1999) *Accident Prevention in Older People – Guidelines for Public Health and Health Promotion*. Newcastle upon Tyne: CPD.

Oakley, A., France-Dawson, M., Fullerton, D. *et al.* (1995) *Review of Effectiveness of Health Promotion Interventions to Prevent Accidents in Older People*. London: University of London.

Orleans, C. T., Jepson, C., Resch, N. and Rimer, B. K. (1994) Quitting motives and barriers among older smokers – the 1986 Adult Use of Tobacco Survey revisited, *Cancer*, 74: 2055–61.

Ponza, M., Ohls, J. C. and Millen, B. E. (1996) *Serving Elders at Risk. The Older Americans Act Nutrition Programs National Evaluation of the Elderly Nutrition Program, 1993 – 1995.* Boston: Mathematica Policy Research, Inc.

Pratt, C. C., Schmall, V. L., Wilson, W. and Benthin, A. (1992) Alcohol problems in later life – evaluation of a model community education program, *Community Mental Health Journal*, 28(4): 327–35.

Prochaska, J. O. and Di Clemente, C. C. (1983) Stages and processes of self change of smoking: toward an integrative model of change, *Journal of Consulting and Clinical Psychology*, 51(3): 390–5.

Raw, M., McNeill, A. and West, R. (1998) Smoking cessation guidelines for health professionals. A guide to effective smoking interventions for the health care system, *Thorax*, 53(suppl. 5): S1–19.

Raw, M., McNeill, A. and West, R. (1999) Smoking cessation: evidence based recommendations for the healthcare system, *British Medical Journal*, 318: 182–5.

Redburn, D. E. and Juretich, M. (1989) Some considerations for using widowed self-help group leaders, *Gerontology and Geriatrics Education*, 9(3): 89–98.

Rimer, B. K. and Orleans, C. T. (1994) Tailoring smoking cessation for older adults, *Cancer*, 74: 2051–4.

Scaf-Klomp, W., van Sonderen, E. and van den Heuvel, W. (1997) Compliance after 17 years of breast cancer screening, *European Journal of Public Health*, 7: 182–7.

Sinclair, H., Bond, C., Lennox, A. S., Silcock, J. and Winfield, A. (1997) An evaluation of a training workshop for pharmacists based on the Stages of Change model of smoking cessation, *Health Education Journal*, 56: 296–312.

Skelton, D. (1999) Physical activity: a unique contribution to effectiveness in practice. Paper presented to Physical Activity and the Prevention and Management of Falls and Accidents conference, Sheffield.

Stead, M., Wimbush, E., Eadie, D. and Teer, P. (1997) A qualitative study of older people's perceptions of ageing and exercise: the implications for health promotion, *Health Education Journal*, 56: 3–16.

Townsend, P. and Davidson, N. (1982) *Inequalities in Health*. London: Penguin.

United States Public Health Service (1992) *Healthy People 2000: National Health Promotion and Disease Prevention Objectives*. Boston, MA: Jones and Bartlett.

Urban, N., Taplin, S. H., Taylor, V. M. *et al*. (1995) Community organisation to promote breast cancer screening among women ages 50–75, *Preventive Medicine* 24(5): 477–84.

Vaughan, S. (1996) Older women's attitudes to breast screening in North Tyneside. Unpublished paper.

Vetter, N. J. and Ford, D. (1990) Smoking prevention among people aged 60 and over: a randomized controlled trial, *Age and Ageing*, 19: 164–8.

Vinokur Kaplan, D., Cibulski, O., Spero, S. and Bergman, S. (1981) 'Oldster-to-oldster': an example of mutual aid through friendly visiting among Israeli elderly, *Journal of Gerontological Social Work*, 4(1): 75–91.

Walker, A. and Maltby, T. (1997) *Ageing Europe*. Buckingham: Open University Press.

Walters, R. (1996) *Health Promotion for Old Age*. London: Eurolink Age.

Ward, M. and Goodman, C. (1995) *Alcohol Problems in Old Age*. Kenley: Staccato Books and Training.

Wolf, S. L., Barnhart, H. X., Kutner, N. G. *et al*. (1996) Reducing frailty and falls in older persons: an investigation of Tai Chi and computerized balance training. Atlanta FICSIT Group. Frailty and injuries: cooperative studies of intervention techniques, *Journal of the American Geriatrics Society*, 44(5): 489–97.

Woods, M. (1997) *Ageing Well in Northern Ireland. Promoting Health with Older People*. Belfast: Age Concern Northern Ireland and Health Promotion Agency Northern Ireland.

2

Inequalities in health-related behaviour among older people

JAY GINN, HELEN COOPER AND
SARA ARBER

The chapter reviews structural inequalities in older people's health-related behaviour and considers the question of how far personal lifestyle is a matter of individual choice or is also influenced by class, gender and age group. Data from the Health Survey for England are used to illustrate inequalities in older people's diet and physical exercise, showing how these health-related behaviours are socially structured.

Increasing longevity has highlighted the importance of 'adding life to years'; that is, promoting health, well-being and functional independence among older people. While life expectancy has often been taken as an indicator of social progress and medical advance, the extension of older people's health expectancy, or years of life free from illness or disability (Bone *et al.* 1995), presents a newer challenge. Yet it is still a concept based on a biomedical model of health. The social model of health is more inclusive, locating individuals in their social context, acknowledging the impact of psychological, social and environmental factors on health and on health-related behaviour. A growing literature on older people's health (Victor 1991; Arber and Ginn 1993, 1998; Sidell 1995) emphasizes the link between their health and their current and previous position in the social structure.

The relative influence on health of individuals' behaviour and of the material and social conditions in which they live has generated much debate (Blane 1985; Macintyre 1986, 1997; Townsend *et al.* 1988a; Wilkinson 1996; Drever and Whitehead 1997). Proponents of the behavioural explanation of inequality in health have emphasized choice and personal responsibility, which tends to blame those in poor health for their condition (Nettleton 1996). Others, however, reject such an individualistic interpretation, arguing that health behaviour is influenced by cultural norms and other factors outside the individual's control. Thus, 'what is attributed to individual choice is in fact substantially shaped by powerful economic and social forces, the goods and facilities that are immediately available and level of income' (Townsend *et al.* 1988b: xiv). Or, as Macintyre (1997: 739) puts it, 'behaviours may be rooted in material conditions or social structural position'. In this interpretation, with which we concur, health-related behaviour is influenced (although not wholly determined) by financial resources, housing, class background, neighbourhood, gender, ethnicity, social networks and relationships (Ginn *et al.* 1997). The success of health promotion in extending healthy life among older people (Berg and Kassels 1990; Kane *et al.* 1990; Hickey and Stilwell 1991; Ageing Well Europe 1996) requires that barriers to healthier living are understood.

The aim of our research on health-related behaviour has been to examine how the lifestyle of older men and women is related to structural factors, as well as to their age and their perception of their own health (Ginn *et al.* 1998; Cooper *et al.* 1999). Health promotion programmes need to take account of socio-economic factors, which can only be tackled by intervention at the level of local or national government.

First, we outline what is known about the health-related behaviour of older people.

Health-related behaviour: variation with age and gender

Physical fitness is crucial to maintaining functional independence for older people (Muir Gray 1985; Fentem *et al.* 1988; Edwards and Larson 1992; Fentem 1992; Pescatello and DiPietro 1993; Haskell 1997). Managing the activities of daily living without assistance depends on having an adequate power–weight ratio and enough joint flexibility. A substantial proportion of people over age 50 are judged to take too little exercise, in that their physical activity is not of sufficient frequency, duration and intensity to produce a health benefit (Skelton *et al.* 1998). A recent qualitative study showed that although older people recognized the value of physical exercise to health, they were deterred by a perceived lack of suitable facilities for older people, lack of transport or money, physical restrictions due to illness, lack of time, a fatalistic attitude to health, especially among men, and a strong perception that physical activity could endanger health 'at our age' (Finch 1997). An older person's confidence in having the physical capability to engage in exercise, termed 'exercise self-efficacy' (Clark 1996: 157), has also been shown to be important in influencing willingness to engage in physical activity.

The Health Survey for England (HSE) report for 1994 shows that physical activity of at least 'moderate' intensity declines more steeply with age for women than men. Thus, in the age group 45–54, 86 per cent of men and 88 per cent of women reported activity which was of at least 'moderate' intensity in the previous four weeks; however, among those aged over 75, the proportions were 47 per cent of men but only 38 per cent of women (Colhoun and Prescott-Clarke 1996: Table 6.3).

An optimum diet, in terms of both quantity of food and balance of types of food consumed, depends on the amount of physical activity. Physical activity generally declines with age, so that dietary habits acquired earlier in life may be ill-adapted to bodily needs in later life, especially for those who previously worked in manual occupations.

Consumption of a variety of food items was compared in the HSE report according to age group. Those aged over 65 were slightly more likely than people of working age to eat white rather than other bread and less likely to use skimmed milk, but for other items their diet was at least as healthy as for younger people (Colhoun and Prescott-Clarke 1996: Tables 7.6–7.18). Women's diets were more healthy than men's, a gender difference thought to arise from the greater importance attached to health by women (Kandrack *et al.* 1991) and to gendered norms of behaviour and self-image; for example, it has been suggested that fruit, vegetables and low-fat foods symbolize lightness and femininity, while meat symbolizes power and masculinity (Twigg 1983).

The health risk of smoking has become increasingly widely accepted, yet at the time when today's older people reached adulthood the links with cancer and other diseases had not been firmly established. At that time, smoking was less socially acceptable among women than men, although changes in gender roles have been accompanied by some convergence in smoking rates of men and women in all but the oldest age groups (Dawes and Goddard 1997).

Current cigarette smoking is less common among those aged over 65 than younger adults; in 1994, a fifth of those aged 65–74 and just over 10 per cent of those aged over 75 smoked, compared with about a third of working age adults (Colhoun and Prescott-Clarke 1996). The prevalence of smoking among older people declined between 1991 and 1994, with the exception of women aged 65–74, who showed a very small increase. The latter probably reflects the tendency for successive cohorts of women to have smoking habits more similar to men's. The decline in prevalence of smoking over time has been due to a rising proportion who have given up smoking, rather than an increase in the proportion who had never smoked (Colhoun and Prescott-Clarke 1996). The Health and Lifestyles Survey, which allows analysis of changes in health and health behaviour of the *same* individuals over time, confirmed that a substantial proportion of people aged over 60 in 1984–5 had given up smoking by 1991–2, 13 per cent of men and 9 per cent of women (Whichelow and Cox 1993). The decrease in smoking was evident in all socio-economic groups to much the same extent, giving grounds for some optimism as to the potential for lifestyle change in later life. Yet the lower rate of smoking decline among older than younger people suggests that the potential for reducing smoking in older age groups has not yet been fully exploited (White 1997).

In sum, older people's lifestyle is more healthy than that of younger people in terms of smoking, similar in terms of diet but poorer in terms of adequate exercise. The latter, however, may partly reflect the increasing proportion with disabilities which restrict their physical activity.

In this chapter, we draw on our recent research on individuals aged 55 and over, in which data from two years of the HSE (1993 and 1994) were used to analyse diet quality, physical activity and current smoking among men and women aged 55 and over according to socio-economic factors and social relationships (Cooper *et al.* 1999). Since the link between smoking and social disadvantage is well established (Dawes and Goddard 1997; Cooper *et al.* 1999), the focus of this chapter is on physical activity and diet quality.

Data and methods

The HSE has been conducted annually since 1991 and was designed to monitor changes in the nation's health. It provides a nationally representative sample of adults aged over 16 living in private households; since 1993 the annual sample size has been approximately 16,000, including over 5500 individuals aged 55 years or more (Bennett *et al.* 1995). For this research, two years of the HSE, 1993 and 1994, were combined, giving a sample size of over 10,000 aged over 55.

The HSE interview includes detailed questions about physical activity in the previous four weeks and usual consumption of foods. Questions on physical activity cover recreational exercise, domestic work, gardening/do-it-yourself (DIY) and walking, with information on frequency of participation and on the effort expended, or intensity of activity; for example, the pace of walking and the type of home-based work is recorded. The HSE provides summary variables measuring total physical activity (including recreational and instrumental activities), in terms of frequency and intensity. Further details concerning the measurement of physical activity are provided elsewhere (Cooper *et al.* 1999).

In nutritional research, assessment of the quality of diet is often based on a food diary, including weights of foods consumed. The HSE, although it does not provide such full information, does include a series of questions on consumption of food items which allow inference to be made about the quality of an individual's diet. Respondents were asked about the type of milk, cereals, bread and spread used, about their means of frying, use of salt and frequency of eating bread, vegetables, fruit, pulses, cakes, sweets and biscuits in the past four weeks. A diet score, in which a higher score represents a healthier diet, was constructed by applying the principles underlying Dowler and Calvert's (1995) Healthy Diet Score. Further details on our method are reported elsewhere (Ginn *et al.* 1998; Cooper *et al.* 1999).

The HSE asks about any longstanding illness and records individuals' own assessment of their general health (very good, good, fair, bad or very bad). As the HSE provides no information on income, a personal deprivation score has been constructed, based on housing tenure, access to a car in the household, access to a telephone in the household, having central heating in the household, whether unemployed and whether reliant on Income Support (see Ginn *et al.* 1998; Cooper *et al.* 1999).

We next examine how two aspects of older people's health behaviour – physical activity and diet quality – vary according to their socio-economic position, gender, marital status and health, while controlling for age group.

Physical activity

Only a small proportion of men and women aged 55 and over had participated in any single form of physical recreation in the previous four weeks.

However, over a quarter participated in at least one of the following: cycling, swimming, dancing, aerobics, exercises such as sit-ups, weight training, running, tennis, squash, badminton and other sporting activities.

Some gender difference in these activities was evident, highlighting the importance of perceptions as to the gender-appropriateness of activities, which may inhibit one gender from participating. Thus cycling was reported by 10 per cent of men but only 6 per cent of women; whereas 4 per cent of women attended aerobics sessions, less than 1 per cent of men did so.

Participation in recreational activities can incur costs, so that lack of material resources, as indicated by the personal deprivation (PD) score, may prevent such activities. The proportion who had been swimming in the previous four weeks declined sharply from the most advantaged group, those having no deprivation according to our index (PD score 0), to the middle group (score 3), with low levels maintained for men and women in the most deprived groups (score 4+). Aerobics attendance followed a similar pattern for women. These associations, which are also evident for the other recreational activities, are consistent with the hypothesis that material deprivation restricts recreational activities. Some recreational activities were clearly associated with class. For example, a greater proportion of older people in the higher socio-economic groups than lower had been swimming in the previous four weeks: 12 per cent of those classed as managers or employers in large organizations or as professionals had been swimming, compared with less than 3 per cent of those classed as unskilled manual workers.

Walking provides an easy and convenient way to improve health, by strengthening muscles and, if the pace is brisk enough, improving aerobic capacity. The proportion walking at least a mile in the previous four weeks, at any pace, fell from 62 per cent of men and women aged 55–59 to 35 per cent of men and 22 per cent of women aged over 80. The proportion of older people who had walked at a brisk or fast pace declined with age from a fifth among those in their late 50s to less than 10 per cent of those aged 70 or over. Gender divergence was apparent after age 65: women's walking (in terms of both the proportion walking at least a mile and the frequency of such walks) decreased linearly with age, while for men no decrease was evident until age 70.

Work done in the home varies in the physical effort required. Accordingly, the HSE distinguishes between light housework (such as food preparation, cooking, laundry) and heavy housework (spring cleaning, moving furniture, cleaning windows, carrying heavy shopping for at least five minutes and scrubbing floors). Figure 2.1 shows the frequency and intensity of men's and women's domestic work in the past four weeks by age group. Not surprisingly, given the gendered norms as to the division of domestic labour, women did more housework than men. For example, among women aged 55–59, nearly all (99 per cent) did some housework, a quarter did only light housework and three-quarters did heavy housework; 16 per cent of women in this age group did heavy housework more than ten times in the past four weeks. Among men in this age group, about 80 per cent did some housework but less than half did heavy housework and only 5 per cent had done heavy housework more than ten times in the previous four weeks.

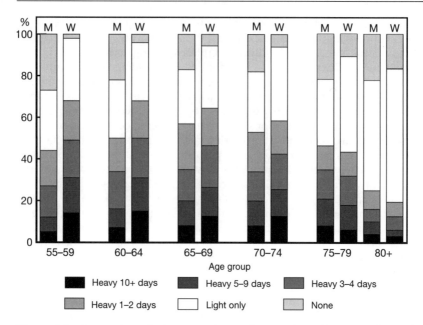

Figure 2.1   Domestic work: frequency in past four weeks and intensity, by gender and age group.
Source: *Health Survey for England*, 1993, 1994 (authors' analysis)

Gender convergence with age in the performance of housework was evident. Whereas women's domestic work declined linearly with age, men's did not. Indeed, the proportion of men doing any housework increased slightly after age 65 to 81 per cent, only declining after age 80. The proportion of men doing heavy domestic work was highest from age 65–74, at just over 50 per cent. By age 75, women's dominance in the performance of heavy domestic work had disappeared, and by age 80, there was very little gender difference in the proportion doing any housework. The gender convergence in housework is likely to reflect the decline with age in the proportion of men and women who were married and a higher prevalence of disability among older women compared with men (Arber and Ginn 1991; Arber and Cooper 1998).

Doing light gardening/DIY was common among both men and women, with over a third of all men and over a third of women under age 75 doing light tasks but no heavy work. Women were less likely than men to do heavy gardening/DIY work. Thus the conventional gender division of labour was evident, with women dominating housework and men gardening and DIY. As expected, the gender division of labour in these home-based physical tasks was primarily among those who were married or cohabiting.

Both the intensity of physical effort and the frequency of activity are important to health. The HSE provides a summary variable indicating the maximum intensity of activity achieved in the previous four weeks – whether none, light, moderate or vigorous – taking into account all the activities considered here, as well as physical work in paid employment, in addition to the frequency of activity at this intensity. Moderate or vigorous activity denotes physical effort which could be expected to benefit health, although the intensity required to maintain or improve health among older people may be less than for younger age groups and less for women than for men.

A gender difference in overall (or 'total') activity was evident within each age group. Those who did not participate in any activity or only in light activities are referred to here as 'sedentary'. Sedentariness increased among men from 22 per cent at age 55–59 to 58 per cent among those aged over 80; for women, the corresponding proportions were 16 and 70 per cent; thus, among those in their late 50s women were less likely to be sedentary than men, but with advancing age women's physical activity declined more steeply than men's.

Physical activity was higher among the better off (see Figure 2.2). Of those in the most advantaged group (PD score 0), only a quarter were sedentary, whereas over half were sedentary in the most disadvantaged group (PD score of 4 or more). Perhaps surprisingly, class, based on each individual's past or current occupation, was not associated with overall physical activity for women, and there was only a slight class gradient in sedentariness for men, from 25 per cent in the highest group (professionals and managers/employers in large organizations) to 35 per cent in the lowest group (unskilled manual). Among women, the minority who had never been employed were much more likely to be sedentary than other women. Educational qualifications, which were held by only half of those aged over 55, showed some association with physical activity. Among those lacking any qualifications, nearly 40 per

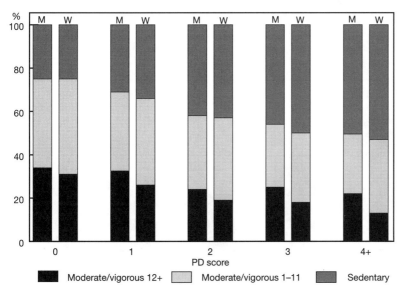

Figure 2.2 Total activity (intensity and frequency) for men and women aged 55 plus by personal deprivation score.
Source: *Health Survey for England*, 1993, 1994 (authors' analysis)

cent were sedentary, compared with under 25 per cent among those whose highest qualification was at least A level or equivalent.

In contrast, the effect of self-assessed health on physical activity was dramatic (see Figure 2.3). Among women who reported their health as 'very good' or 'good', three-quarters had engaged in moderate or vigorous activity in the previous four weeks, compared with only 14 per cent among those who said their health was 'very bad'. The gender difference in physical activity noted above remained statistically significant for those with good health ($p < 0.001$) and among those reporting their health as 'fair' ($p < 0.05$) but not among those reporting 'bad' or 'very bad' health.

The relationship between self-assessed health and physical activity was not simply due to a decline in health with age; the adverse effect of poor self-assessed health on activity was evident within each age group (not shown). For example, among men in the youngest age group (55–59) sedentariness ranged from 12 per cent where health was reported as 'very good/good' to 64 per cent where it was 'bad/very bad'. Self-rated health was more important than age in influencing physical activity; for example, even in the oldest age group (over 80) the majority of men reporting very good/good health were active at a moderate or vigorous level. Advancing age was still associated with lower activity after controlling for self-assessed health. The association between self-assessed health and physical activity was more pronounced for men than for women.

The analysis of physical activity has shown that poor self-rated health is a more important predictor of a sedentary lifestyle than material deprivation, low social class, lack of education or chronological age; and that current material living standards have a greater impact on physical activity than class or educational level.

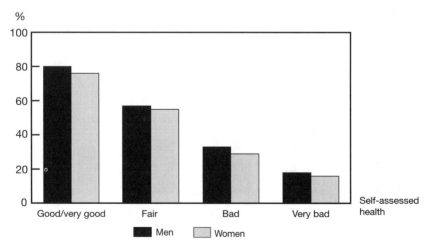

Figure 2.3   Percentage activity at a moderate or vigorous level by self-assessed health: men and women aged 55 plus.
Source: *Health Survey for England*, 1993, 1994 (authors' analysis)

Multivariate analysis using logistic regression showed that age group, self-assessed health, chronic health status, and material resources were each independently associated with sedentariness; for men, educational qualifications were also relevant, and for women, those who had never been employed were more likely to be sedentary.

In order to illustrate the relative influence of health, age group and material resources on physical activity, the odds ratios of sedentariness are shown in Figure 2.4 for these variables. Odds ratios represent the odds of sedentariness for individuals in each category of a variable compared with the odds for those in the reference category, where the odds are defined as 1.00. For men reporting very bad health, the odds of being sedentary were nearly 16 times greater than for the reference group (reporting very good/good health). Men aged 80 plus had an odds ratio of sedentariness over four times higher than men aged 55–59 and men in the most materially disadvantaged group (PD score of 4 or more) had an odds ratio of nearly 2. For women, however, the effect of very bad health was not much greater than the effect of being aged over 80, compared with the respective reference groups. The odds of sedentariness for men and women cannot be compared directly in this analysis, since it was carried out separately for each sex.

In summary, older women's level of physical activity was lower than men's in each age group and declined more steeply with age. Poor self-assessed health was a more important influence on older men's physical activity than ageing but, for older women, the separate effects of ageing and poor health were of similar importance in reducing physical activity. For both men and women, sedentariness was associated with living in poor material circumstances.

Diet quality

We next turn to variation in older people's diet. A summary diet score was computed for each individual from his or her reported consumption of different foods and the score was used as an indicator of diet quality. A large negative score indicates an unhealthy diet, high in sugar, cakes, biscuits, sweets, salt and saturated fats and low in fruit, vegetables, pulses, and fibre-rich foods, while a positive score represents a healthier diet. Diet quality was analysed according to gender, socio-economic position, marital status and health, while controlling for age group.

For men and women aged 55 and over, diet scores ranged from −19 to +18, with a mean value of 0.32. The quality of diet was significantly better among older women than men; women's mean score was 1.10, men's −0.66, and the gender difference was maintained within each age group (see Figure 2.5). Diet quality declined linearly with age for both men and women. Among the very old, aged over 80, both men and women had poorer than average diets.

As expected, those who were married had a better diet than those who were widowed or single, and women's diets were better than men's within each marital status category (not shown). For men, the positive effect of marriage persisted after controlling for age group, suggesting that having a

(a)   Odds ratio

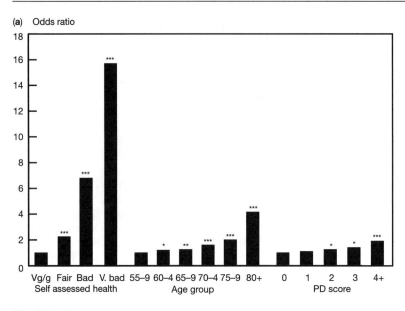

(b)   Odds ratio

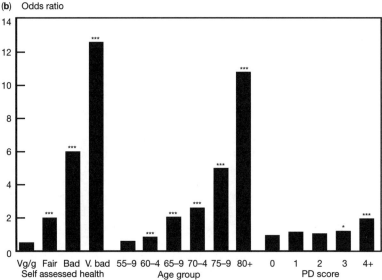

Statistical significance of difference of the odds ratio from reference category: *** *p* < .001, ** *p* < .01, * *p* < .05

Figure 2.4   Odds ratios of sedentariness for age group, general health and personal deprivation score. **(a)** Men aged 55 plus; **(b)** women aged 55 plus.
Source: *Health Survey for England*, 1993, 1994 (authors' analysis)

wife promotes better shopping, cooking and eating practices. The most unhealthy diets were found among single and widowed men.

Class, based on the individual's current or last occupational group, was

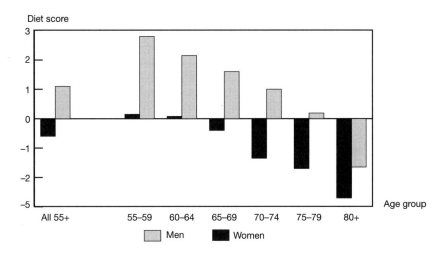

Figure 2.5 Diet quality by age group: men and women aged 55 plus.
Source: *Health Survey for England*, 1993, 1994 (authors' analysis)

associated with diet score. For example, women in the professional/managerial group had a mean diet score of 3.6, compared with −0.2 for women previously in unskilled manual occupations (not shown).

The difference in diet according to the personal deprivation score was even greater than for class; women in the most materially advantaged group (PD score 0) had a diet score of 2.7, compared with −2.3 for the most materially deprived women with a PD score of 4 or more, while for men the corresponding diet scores were 0.5 and −4.1 (see Figure 2.6).

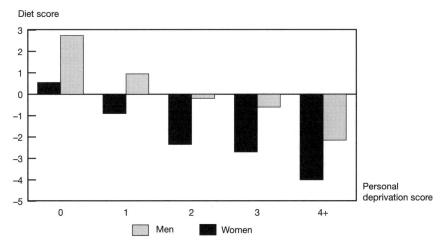

Figure 2.6 Diet quality by personal deprivation score: men and women aged 55 plus.
Source: *Health Survey for England*, 1993, 1994 (authors' analysis).

Multivariate analysis, using logistic regression, allowed the separate effects on diet quality of the above variables to be assessed. Material deprivation, low social class and older age each had strong, and largely independent, effects, increasing the likelihood of a poorer than average diet score. Women living alone had a significantly better diet quality than those who were married. Although those with poor self-assessed health were more likely to have a worse than average diet than those in good health, longstanding illness was associated with a healthier diet; this may reflect a response to medical advice concerning management of a chronic condition.

Figure 2.7 shows the odds ratios of a poorer than average diet, for age group and personal deprivation score, derived from the logistic regression analyses. The effect of material deprivation was greater than that of age, for both men and women. For example, among the most disadvantaged men (PD score of 4 or more), the odds of a poorer than average diet were nearly 3.7 times the odds for the most advantaged (the reference group, odds defined as 1.00); among men aged over 80, the odds ratio was 2.2, compared with men aged 55–59 (the reference group).

To summarize, older women's diets were markedly better than older men's but for both men and women poor diet quality was associated with older age and with poorer socio-economic circumstances.

Discussion

The aim of this chapter was to examine the influence of socially created circumstances, particularly current material resources, social class and educational level, on older people's health behaviour. The pattern of effects of these factors was similar for physical activity and diet quality: a disadvantaged position in the social structure was clearly associated with less healthy behaviour. Both sedentariness and poor diet were significantly more likely among those who were materially deprived and those in lower social classes, after taking account of the effects of age and health.

The effect of material deprivation on physical activity may reflect several barriers, including the costs of participating in recreational activities and of transport, cramped accommodation and lack of a garden. The most deprived older people are also more likely to live in a neighbourhood which is unsafe and unsuitable for walking, in terms of both the built and the social environment. The decline in diet quality with deteriorating material circumstances is also likely to reflect cost considerations, although the separate association of poor diet with low occupational class indicates that class-related social norms may play a part in dietary habits.

Ageing was associated with increasing sedentariness, as expected, but also with a worsening diet quality. This suggests that age-linked physical difficulties in shopping, or in preparing and eating certain foods, may limit the available choices. However, those in the younger age groups may also have better information as to the requirements of a healthy diet. Those with a chronic illness were more likely to be sedentary than those without, but chronic ill-health seems to encourage older men and women to take more care of themselves, in terms of diet. Poor self-assessed health constitutes a

(a) Odds ratio

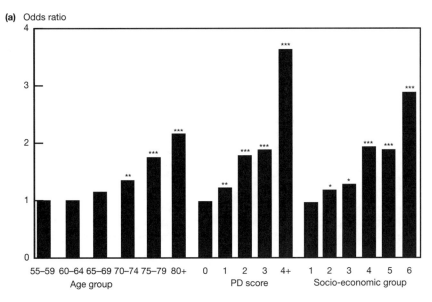

(b) Odds ratio

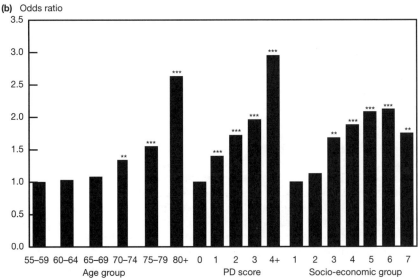

Socio-economic category (SEC)
1 Managers/employers in large organization/professionals.
2 Managers/employers in small organization/intermediate
  non-manual ancillary.
3 Junior non-manual.

4 Skilled manual/supervisory, farmers (own account).
5 Semi-skilled manual/personal service/agricultural.
6 Unskilled manual.
7 Never employed.

Excluded: inadequate description, armed forces.

Statistical significance of difference of the odds ratio from reference category: *** $p < .001$, ** $p < .01$, * $p < .05$

Figure 2.7   Odds ratios of poorer than average diet for age group, personal deprivation score and socio-economic group. **(a)** Men aged 55 plus; **(b)** women aged 55 plus.
Source: *Health Survey for England*, 1993, 1994 (authors' analysis)

major barrier to physical activity, especially for older men, far outweighing the effect of chronological age. Thus we conclude that poor health status rather than ageing *per se* is the primary influence in restricting physical activity. Poor health status is also weakly associated with a poorer diet.

Gender had mixed effects on health behaviour, in that older women's physical activity was less in all types of activity except domestic work, but their diet quality was much better than men's. Among women, those living alone were more likely to have a healthy diet than those who were married, after taking account of other variables. This suggests that where women have sole control of their diet, it is likely to be healthier than where meals are shared with others. For men, in contrast, marriage was associated with a better diet, although this relationship no longer held after controlling for age, health, class and material resources.

Further research is required to illuminate the processes through which health-damaging behaviour is linked to material deprivation and low class and is more likely among men. A key concern must be to disentangle the indirect effects of class and material resources on health (through their influence on health behaviour) from their more direct effects on health.

Conclusions: implications for health promotion among older people

Those working to promote more healthy lifestyles among older people need to consider the extent to which individuals are able to act upon their knowledge of what constitutes healthy behaviour and how financial, social and physical barriers to healthier living can be minimized. Diet and exercise habits may be amenable to change, provided the factors preventing change are understood and addressed by government and local initiatives.

Information on healthy lifestyles is valuable but not sufficient. For example, the means to obtain affordable, healthy foods locally (or to have them delivered), as well as the ability to manage simple cooking, may be as important as knowledge of dietary needs. Some communities organize wholesale food co-ops to buy and distribute good quality fresh food among themselves, although some local food projects are more successful than others (McGlone *et al.* 1999); such initiatives could be facilitated by local government and older people could be encouraged to participate. Higher dietary standards in meals-on-wheels and in food served in luncheon clubs for older people would help to ensure a balanced diet for those too frail to shop and cook for themselves.

A wish list for promoting physical exercise among older people could include, for those in reasonable health:

- provision of free facilities for older people at swimming baths and leisure centres;
- dancing clubs with free classes;
- assistance in forming local rambling groups where these are lacking;
- improvements to the urban environment, with a network of safe, well lit pedestrian walkways and parks.

For those with restricted mobility, heart conditions and other chronic illnesses, suitable physical activity can improve balance and flexibility and contribute to general well-being. More resources in the NHS for physiotherapy, including home visits, could remobilize those whose inactivity is health-related, paying dividends in increased functional independence. Health care professionals have a crucial role in challenging fatalistic attitudes in society, in the NHS and in older people themselves concerning ageing and health. The notion that poor health is inevitable in later life may inhibit provision of therapy; it also undermines older people's motivation to improve their lifestyle.

Although health promotion programmes have an important contribution to make, the influence of social disadvantage on older people's health-related behaviour highlights the need for social policy to address poverty in later life. Currently, the decline in the basic state pension relative to average earnings is widening the income gap between older people who lack any private pension (two-thirds of older women) and the rest of society (Ginn and Arber 1999). Raising the basic pension may be an effective way to improve older people's health and health behaviour: 'it is entirely possible that the most efficient way to reduce the disease burden associated with poor health behaviours . . . is to improve the socioeconomic conditions which generate them' (Lynch *et al.* 1997: 817).

References

Ageing Well Europe (1996) *A European Programme of Health Promotion for and with Older People*. London: Ageing Well Europe.

Arber, S. and Cooper, H. (1998) Gender differences in health in later life: the new paradox?, *Social Science and Medicine*, 48: 61–76.

Arber, S. and Ginn, J. (1991) *Gender and Later Life: A Sociological Analysis of Resources and Constraints*. London: Sage.

Arber, S. and Ginn, J. (1993) Gender and inequalities in health in later life, *Social Science and Medicine,* special issue on women, men and health, 36(1): 33–46.

Arber, S. and Ginn, J. (1998) Health and illness in later life, in D. Field and S. Taylor (eds) *Sociological Perspectives on Health and Illness*. London: Blackwell Scientific.

Bennett, N., Dodd, T., Glatley, J., Freeth, S. and Boiling, K. (1995) *Health Survey for England 1993*. Social Survey Division, OPCS. London: HMSO.

Berg, R. and Cassells, J. (1990) *The Second Fifty Years: Promoting Health and Preventing Disability*. Washington, DC: National Academy Press.

Blane, D. (1985) An assessment of the Black Report's 'explanations' of health inequalities, *Sociology of Health and Illness*, 7(3): 423–45.

Bone, M., Bebbington, A., Jagger, C., Morgan, K. and Nicolaas, G. (1995) *Health Expectancy and Its Uses*. London: HMSO.

Clark, D. (1996) Age, socioeconomic status and exercise self-efficacy, *The Gerontologist*, 36(2): 157–64.

Colhoun, H. and Prescott-Clarke, P. (eds) (1996) *Health Survey for England 1994*. London: HMSO.

Cooper, H., Ginn, J. and Arber, S. (1999) *Health Related Behaviour and Attitudes of Older People: A Secondary Analysis of National Datasets*. London: Health Education Authority.

Dawes, F. and Goddard, E. (1997) *Smoking-related Behaviour and Attitudes*. London: Stationery Office.

Dowier, E. and Calvert, C. (1995) *Nutrition and Diet in Lone Parent Families in London.* London: Family Policy Study Centre.

Drever, F. and Whitehead, M. (eds) (1997) *Health Inequalities: Decennial Supplement.* London: Stationery Office.

Edwards, K. and Larson, E. (1992) Benefits of exercise for older people, *Clinical Geriatric Medicine,* 8: 35–52.

Fentem, P. (1992) Exercise in prevention of disease, *British Medical Bulletin,* 48(3): 630–50.

Fentem, P., Bassey, E. and Turnbull, N. (1988) *The New Case for Exercise.* London: HEA.

Finch, H. (1997) *Physical Activity 'at our age'. Qualitative Research among People over the Age of 50.* London: HEA.

Ginn, J. and Arber, S. (1999) Changing patterns of pension inequality: the shift from state to private sources, *Ageing and Society,* 19(3): 319–42.

Ginn, J., Arber, S. and Cooper, H. (1997) *Researching Older People's Health Needs and Health Promotion Issues.* London: HEA.

Ginn, J., Arber, S. and Cooper, H. (1998) Inequalities in older people's health behaviour: Effect of structural factors and social relationships', *Journal of Contemporary Health,* special issue on health inequalities, (7): 77–82.

Haskell, W. (1997) Personal health benefits of exercise for older people. Research into Ageing's 21st Anniversary lecture, presented at the Active for Later Life Conference, Birmingham.

Hickey, T. and Stilwell, D. (1991) Health promotion for older people: all is not well, *The Gerontologist,* 31(6): 822–9.

Kandrack, M., Grant, K. and Segall, A. (1991) Gender differences in health related behaviour: some unanswered questions, *Social Science and Medicine,* 32: 579.

Kane, R., Grimley-Evans, G. and Macfadyen, D. (eds) (1990) *Improving the Health of Older People: A World View.* Oxford: Oxford University Press.

Lynch, J., Kaplan, G. and Salonen, J. (1997) Why do poor people behave poorly? Variation in adult health behaviours and psychosocial characteristics by stages of the socioeconomic lifecourse, *Social Science and Medicine,* 44(6): 809–19.

McGlone, P., Dobson, B., Dowier, E. and Nelson, M. (1999) *Food Projects and How They Work.* York: JRF.

Macintyre, S. (1986) The patterning of health by social position in contemporary Britain: directions for sociological research, *Social Science and Medicine,* 23(4): 393–415.

Macintyre, S. (1997) The Black Report and beyond: what are the issues?, *Social Science and Medicine,* special issue on health inequalities in modern societies and beyond, 44(6): 723–45.

Muir Gray, J. (1985) The risks of inactivity, in J. Muir Gray (ed.) *Prevention of Disease in the Elderly.* Edinburgh: Churchill Livingstone.

Pescatello, L. and DiPietro, L. (1993) Physical activities in older adults: an overview of health benefits, *Sports Medicine,* 15(6): 353–64.

Sidell, M. (1995) *Health in Old Age: Myth, Mystery and Management.* Buckingham: Open University Press.

Skelton, D., Young, A., Walker, A. and Hoinville, E. (1998) *Physical Activity in Later Life. Further Analysis of the Allied Dunbar National Fitness Survey and the Health Education Authority National Survey of Activity and Health.* London: University Department of Geriatric Medicine and Royal Free Hospital School of Medicine.

Townsend, P., Davidson, N. and Whitehead, M. (1988a) *Inequalities in Health: The Black Report and the Health Divide.* London: Penguin.

Townsend, P., Phillimore, P. and Beattie, A. (1988b) *Health and Deprivation. Inequality and the North.* London: Croom Helm.

Twigg, J. (1983) Vegetarianism and the meanings of meat, in A. Murcott (ed.) *The Sociology of Food and Eating*. Aldershot: Gower.

Victor, C. (1991) Continuity or change: inequalities in health in later life, *Ageing and Society*, 11(1): 23–39.

Whichelow, M. and Cox, B. (1993) Alterations in smoking patterns, in B. Cox, F. Huppert and M. Whichelow (eds) *The Health and Lifestyle Survey: Seven Years On*. Aldershot: Dartmouth.

White, C. (1997) Older smokers are left out of anti-smoking policies, *British Medical Journal*, 315(7115): 1–2.

Wilkinson, R. (1996) *Unhealthy Societies*. Oxford: Blackwell.

3

Intergenerational health promotion and active citizenship

___ GILLIAN GRANVILLE _____

This chapter begins with a discussion about citizenship, the way this concept developed in the political climate of the 1990s and the relevance it has to health and well-being. It then moves on to discuss how citizenship forms the framework for understanding the dynamics that take place within the intergenerational exchange, and how models of active citizenship and intergenerational working, when they operate positively, are health-promoting activities in themselves. The next part of the chapter describes a practical piece of work carried out by the Beth Johnson Foundation in North Staffordshire, in which old and young people came together to look at issues of concern in their neighbourhood, and the potential health gains this had for the whole community. The chapter concludes with a discussion on the lessons learnt from such an approach and the potential of intergenerational models to act as catalysts for social change in the context of health and health promotion.

Citizenship

Since the beginning of the 1990s, there has been a developing interest in the United Kingdom in the notion of citizenship and an encouragement for people to take an active role in determining their lives. Initially, the Citizen's Charter programme (Cabinet Office 1991), launched by the Conservative government in the early 1990s, was primarily concerned with consumer rights in the public services and was set against the belief that people had an obligation to take individual responsibility for their lives.

A decade later, there has been increasing unease about a society that has become one of self-interest, and that shows a decline in class solidarity and mutual self-help (Crewe 1997: 2). The current government's response has been to promote national strategies that attempt to bring those groups that have been excluded by society back into mainstream and to develop an inclusive environment that supports all its citizens. Tony Blair, in the introduction to the Social Exclusion Unit's third report about neighbourhood renewal, states:

> Over the last two decades the gap between these 'worst estates' and the rest of the country has grown. It has left us with a situation that no civilised country should tolerate. It is simply not acceptable that so many children go to school hungry, or that so many teenagers grow up with no real prospect of a job and that so many pensioners are afraid to go out of their homes. It shames the nation, it wastes lives and we all have to pay the costs of dependency and social division.
>
> (Social Exclusion Unit 1998: 7)

Underpinning these government strategies for a more inclusive society has been the need to empower individuals and local communities to be part of shaping their futures through developing the concept of citizenship. Citizenship is commonly understood in two ways:

- Grounded in democracy and civil rights in a society whose choices are based on private preferences, the aggregation of which produces the greatest happiness for the greatest number.
- Members of a community with shared traditions bound to each other by ties of mutual obligation and common purpose (Crewe 1997: 4).

This context of citizenship in Britain today has moved away from consumer rights and individualism, towards a responsibility for people to be involved in supporting others, in order to create an interdependent and caring society for all its members. This can be done through involvement in the democratic process and in giving to others through, for example, voluntary activity.

Education in citizenship

One key way the government has striven to promote citizenship and create change, has been to introduce it into the National Curriculum in schools, so that young people are encouraged to be active citizens from an early stage in their education. The Advisory Group set up by the government in November 1997 had as its purpose 'To provide advice on effective education for citizenship in schools', and its final report (Qualifications and Curriculum Authority 1998) found: 'There were worrying levels of apathy, ignorance and cynicism about political and public life and also involvement in neighbourhood and community affairs.' It sees the benefits for pupils of citizenship education as being 'empower[ing] them to participate in society effectively as active, informed, critical and responsible citizens of our democracy and of the wider world.'

Citizenship and health

Alongside the developments in education, there have been other initiatives which have sought to involve all sections of the community in improving their health and well-being. The changes in the National Health Service

(Department of Health 1997), the green paper *Our Healthier Nation* (Department of Health 1998a), Health Action Zones and Healthy Living Centres (Department of Health 1998b) are all underpinned by the concept of citizenship and the need for people to become involved in finding solutions to improve the health of themselves and their communities. Similarly, the proposals to modernize local government and initiatives such as Better Government for Older People (Dunning 1999) have sought to encourage all age groups to take responsibility and to work in partnership with government and local authorities to build a more inclusive society. Active citizenship indicates a health-promoting way of life by empowering people within their communities to identify and assert their needs

The King's Fund programme of citizens' juries is one example of an initiative to examine the role of citizens' juries as a tool to involve local people in decision-making about health care (Davies *et al.* 1998). It saw it as an opportunity to investigate the role of the citizen in health care policy and planning. The lessons learnt from that programme (McIver 1998) will help to inform how to engage effectively with people in their communities, and how to take forward the notion of citizenship in order to sustain the necessary commitment required for this process of social change.

The intergenerational exchange

The shift in society towards a need to become more socially inclusive, and to encourage people to act as good citizens by taking a responsible role in their community, is very timely for the development of models of intergenerational exchange. The concept underpinning this relationship is the bringing together of two discriminated groups in our society, who for various reasons have become separated from each other. The process of bringing them together for the purposes of mutual benefit fosters and promotes the whole notion of citizenship. Individuals participate in activities which support and enhance the lives of each group, as well as the wider communities they live in (Newman *et al.* 1997). Intergenerational work enables positive social exchanges and mutual support between generations, which improves individual and collective social health. I develop this idea in more detail before moving on to describe a practical piece of work which demonstrated how an intergenerational programme sought to improve the health of its community through a model of active citizenship.

What is meant by 'intergenerational'?

One of the reasons why intergenerational programmes are not always recognized for their potential power as models of social change is the lack of clarity as to what it means. There are several differing viewpoints and more debate is required, to develop an understanding of which generations are involved and what is their particular roles. There are potential conflicts with a way of working which itself may exclude others. At the Beth Johnson Foundation, we are currently defining 'intergenerational' as work with generations who are separated by a generation between, and where there is no biological connection. This definition was drawn up at an international seminar in Dortmund in April 1999, where a number of organizations from across the world that are involved in intergenerational activities met to develop a theoretical understanding of the work. It primarily means working with children and young people and those who are classed as older adults, and who are usually not involved in paid economic activity. It also means we recognize there is a difference between grandparent–grandchild relationships and those where there is no family tie.

The confusion occurs when 'intergenerational' is taken to mean 'multi-generational' activity, when no distinction is made between the different roles that each offers to the process. In the context of the definition of the older and younger generations coming together in planned activities, the middle generation has a very important role in facilitating the process and enabling the exchange to take place (Newman and Marks 1980). This can be in various ways; for example, as parents, teachers and paid community workers. If we accept that the generations have become disconnected from each other, then it is necessary for there to be mechanisms to bring them back together, and in this way the middle generation has a significant and important part to play.

Disconnection of the generations

The past two to three decades in the Western world, and particularly in the United States and the United Kingdom, the generations have become progressively disconnected from each other at an individual, family and community level due to a number of circumstances, which has meant that the natural relationship between them has been affected, and suspicion of and uncertainty between each other has been generated. These disconnections include smaller families, geographical distance between family members, divorce, single-parent households and the different expectations of working women (Arber and Evandrou 1993). Alongside these changing family structures has been the development of age-segregated activities and living arrangements, which have further distanced the old and young from each other.

These disconnections have been exaggerated by, or perhaps are a consequence of, the lack of value society places on its older and younger members. They have become further excluded from mainstream opportunities, and age discrimination abounds in employment, education and health and social care (Phillipson 1998). Old age is considered undesirable and a time of decline which causes a drain on resources. Young people are seen as non-contributors to the economy, disenfranchised from society and blamed for being irresponsible and the cause of social ills. The distance developed between the generations has meant that older people lose their natural wish to guide and nurture the young, and the young miss the experience and understanding of a person who has lived through a period of time. In intergenerational programmes, both groups, when they come together, recognize their similarities and the way they are excluded from society. This creates a unique synergy between them, which bonds and strengthens them, developing mutual benefit, and feelings of reciprocity and respect for each other (Newman *et al.* 1997).

Intergenerational programmes

In order for this synergy to occur and for its potential to be realized as a model of social change, intergenerational programmes need to contain certain elements. If the requirements are not clear, there is a danger that the process can reinforce and perpetuate the very concerns it is seeking to avoid. It is helpful to divide programmes, which are the practical delivery of intergenerational activity, into three models and to be clear which model is being used in the particular programme (McCrea and Smith 1997). The three models are:

- older people giving a service to children and youth;
- children and youth serving older people;
- children, youth and older people serving together.

The programmes need to be well planned activities, integral to the work of the organization they are involved in and not accidental or one-off occasions. There is a danger in considering that because this is a natural relationship, it does not need time, resources and careful planning. It has to be understood by everyone in the process, and to bring value and mutual benefit to both generations. The programmes also need to show an improvement in the quality of life for both groups and, through that, a benefit to everyone.

The evaluation of intergenerational programmes will show if they have reached their intended outcomes and they need to be widely disseminated through a number of different disciplines. Alongside these, a wider research agenda needs to be developed to further our understanding of the processes involved, and the way these models work towards a more socially inclusive society which values all ages.

The European Year of Older People and Solidarity between Generations in 1993 acted as a catalyst for a range of intergenerational projects to develop in the United Kingdom. These have often been attractive add-ons to existing work, or free-standing, without any wider debate of their value to society and as agents of change. This contrasts with the situation in the United States, which has, for the past 25 years, been developing intergenerational studies as an academic discipline with a sound knowledge base. The work of Sally Newman, Executive Director at Generations Together at the University of Pittsburgh, has been particularly significant (Newman *et al*. 1997). There is now a move to see how the American approach may have relevance in other countries and cultures throughout the world, through seminars such as the Dortmund meeting in 1999.

The chapter now continues with a practical example of an intergenerational programme in the United Kingdom, in which younger and older people served together to improve the health of their local community.

Intergenerational community action

The Beth Johnson Foundation is a charitable trust based in North Staffordshire, which has an international reputation, primarily in the field of gerontology, for its action research projects. During its 27-year history, it has sought to be at the forefront of ageing issues and is particularly known for its work on healthy ageing (Bernard 2000) and advocacy (Ivers 1994). Its history of innovation and responsible risk-taking has been documented elsewhere (Granville 1998), and at the end of the 1990s the Foundation was seeking new ways to improve the quality of life for people as they age. One way to do that is through developing a theoretical and practical understanding of the intergenerational exchange, and the implications of the model for social change.

The intergenerational programme described here evolved from a prior piece of work at the Foundation between 1993 and 1996 (SCIPSHA: Senior Citizens Involved in Public Services, Health and Advocacy), which sought to demonstrate a model for involving older people in decisions which they considered were important to their lives. It was a process model, concerned with the way older people may be able to influence the decision-makers about changes in their neighbourhoods, and was grounded in a community development approach. The effectiveness of the model was demonstrated by the many successful outcomes the groups achieved in gaining access to the decision-makers and improving their neighbourhoods, and in the way citizenship was promoted by older people, in changing their community for the benefit of all. It also showed that older people defined health in a holistic way, which included their mental and social well-being, and recognized the importance of public health issues in promoting good health.

The model for engagement was through the formation of small groups, facilitated by a paid worker from the Foundation, who met in their neighbourhoods and decided on their concerns. It became apparent at an early stage of discussions that the issues that concerned older people were the same that worried the younger members of the community, and that they could perhaps work together to influence change.

In 1997, with funding from Charity Projects, the Phoenix Fund and the Foundation's own resources, an intergenerational coordinator was appointed to test out the potential of an intergenerational approach to community action. Alongside this, a mentoring programme was developed as a model of older people serving young people, and this has since been evaluated (Ellis 1998). This chapter focuses on the community action programme.

The community action groups

Four groups were formed in neighbourhoods around North Staffordshire, in the West Midlands Region of England. As stated above, it is a complex and detailed process to bring the generations together effectively, particularly in communities where they are mistrusted by each other. Many of the older people expressed fear of young people and perceived them as being irresponsible and uncaring. The younger people were bewildered at times by the reactions of older people towards them, but were also influenced by the negative stereotypes, fuelled by the media, of old age.

A community development model was used, based on the experience of the SCIPSHA project, to locate older people who may wish to be involved with a group of young people in improving their local community. Despite what has been said about mistrust, there were a number of older people who were willing to give it a try. This reinforced our beliefs that older people have a natural desire to support young people and that the disconnected community is artificial to its members. The older people met as a single generation group on two or three occasions as a way of preparation, and to develop a mutual understanding of how they would interact with the younger generation. The group offered opportunities for people to voice their prejudices and to establish a way of working with young people that would not reinforce negative stereotypes of each other.

The local secondary schools were approached as a way of reaching the younger members. This is not necessarily the only route to engage with young people, and youth workers were often drawn into the process. The schools, however, were very effective in facilitating the Foundation to be involved and saw themselves as very much part of the local community. In this way, the involvement of the generation in between the two age groups was essential in enabling the process to develop. Most of the young students who joined the three groups were in the last two years of secondary school (14–16-year-olds) and did so voluntarily; with a few it was part of their Duke of Edinburgh Awards for community service, and for some it was a part of the school's personal and social education programme.

The intergenerational coordinator met the young people as a single generation group, in the same way she had met the older ones. They had the opportunity to talk through their experiences of older people other than their grandparents, to talk about stereotypes and to share their concerns as to how the group would function.

The groups began meeting as an intergenerational activity on a regular basis, approximately monthly throughout the school year. The times of the meetings varied between in-school time, lunchtimes or after school, and the venues also varied a little, but often the schools presented the most acceptable environment for everyone. The groups were arranged so that there were approximately even numbers of the generations, and the totals ranged between 16 and 20 in each of the three groups. The young people were divided fairly evenly by gender, but the older people were made up predominantly of women, which is an issue the Foundation would like to examine more closely in any future work. There were no members of black or ethnic minority populations because there are very few living in the communities in which the groups were working.

In the early meetings, time was spent getting to know each other as individuals, as well as establishing ground rules for the way the group would operate. Different ways of working were used, such as small group work, wordstorming and individual feedback. Great care was exercised to ensure that stereotypes were not reinforced, by, for example, the older people not always taking a lead in discussions, or the younger members always making the tea. However, respect was fostered between the generations through a recognition of some of the physical frailty that comes with age, such as hearing impairment and use of a walking stick, and the needs of the younger ones were also recognized and respected, such as their examination pressures.

The issues for the groups

The generations worked together in the groups to decide on their concerns for the community, and, as stated above, they were surprised that they had the same problems. Neither group liked walking through a dismal subway and both were concerned at the level of vandalism in a local park. They both were dissatisfied with the concessionary fares on the local buses and all disliked the amount of litter in the neighbourhoods. The young people also found considerable support for their own issues and the willingness of the older people to work with them to find solutions. The older people were outraged by the way all young people were being treated at a local leisure centre, purely because of their age. Another group recognized how few social facilities there were available for young people compared with when they were younger, and felt it was unjust. The connections to health showed in their wishes for a cleaner neighbourhood, and an improvement in physical and social activities. They felt that their mental health was affected through fear of personal safety and crime, and the stress they all found from a segregated community. They recognized the pressures on the middle generation and the limitations of the support they could offer, because of their concerns with economic activity.

The process of influence

The regular meetings enabled the groups to develop a clear identity and they learnt to work together in a structured way. Agendas and minutes were used to mirror the format of official meetings so that everyone became more comfortable with that approach. Training focused on skill development and role play was used to enhance communication skills in negotiation and assertiveness. The style the group wanted to adopt was one of persuasion and bringing people on their side rather than one of confrontation.

Visits were made to observe formal meetings, such as those held at the local district and county councils, which helped their understanding of the democratic processes. It provided them with an opportunity to meet local politicians and to identify the key people who held the power.

Knowledge about their particular concerns was learnt within the safety of the group, so they developed their own understanding of the problem before meeting the decision-makers, and were able to argue their case from a base of knowledge. The groups rehearsed the approaches they would take before meeting officials, so they felt prepared and informed.

Finally, a media strategy was agreed in which the groups understood that it was more effective to avoid sensationalism, which could alienate those it wished to influence, and instead to use the media to illustrate positive co-operation and successful outcomes. It was also important to try to educate the media in understanding intergenerational cooperation, so they did not present the stereotypes of old and young which we were seeking to avoid.

Evaluation

This intergenerational programme of old and young people coming together to serve their community has recently undergone an evaluation (Beth Johnson Foundation 2000). The evaluation sought to answer two questions:

- Does this intergenerational partnership act as a change agent in the local community?
- Is there any perceived change of attitude between the generations, and in the way they are perceived by others?

The groups were effective in making changes in their neighbourhoods. For example, the leisure centre created a membership card for the use of young people, the local bus service is improving the way it administers its concessionary fares and the local authority is consulting with one of the action groups on its facilities in the town. The decision-makers were able to recognize the power of two age groups, who appear to be at odds with each other, coming together and agreeing on the same issues in their community. It is particularly powerful when it is from two groups who often feel excluded, with their needs disregarded by the authorities.

However, the greatest changes have been in how the age groups perceived each other, and the way in which this led to a deeper understanding of each other's needs. They realized that, although both groups had significant contact with grandchildren or grandparents, their negative attitudes to each other came from living in the community. They recognized the similarities between themselves. One young woman said: 'We like the same things, such as meeting together with your friends in groups, either at the Darby and Joan Club or in the park.' The older group members deepened their respect for young people and the many difficult issues and pressures they faced. The young people felt valued by the older people's support for their concerns, and the older members were impressed by the responsible attitudes and aspirations of this generation of young people. Both groups also expressed the difference in their relationship, as against others they had with other generations, in that they all felt equal and alongside each other in facing concerns. It was clear that the decision-makers and others who came into contact with the intergenerational groups were also surprised to observe this relationship of mutual respect, in what are often thought of as two generations with opposing needs.

Discussion

This chapter has examined a model of citizenship in which two generations, often disconnected from each other in our society, came together to serve their local community. It reinforces the notion of citizenship, where a group in a community had a common purpose to improve the situation for its members. For example, developing more leisure facilities for the young gave them a meaningful activity, while making them less threatening to older people and therefore improving the mental health of all concerned. Through an understanding of each other, both age groups saw beyond the negative stereotypes of socially excluded groups and found individual personalities that they liked and respected.

Active citizenship was further enhanced by the potential of the young people to show a social responsibility to the frailty that may occur with old age, and the older members showed a responsibility to the young people by supporting and championing their needs.

This model of community action also fostered an understanding of democracy, how it operated to the good of others and the importance of being involved in the process. It is clear from the groups' experiences that many of their issues were only at the beginning of making social changes, and that the democratic processes were slow and tedious at times. However, this did not detract from the groups' viability and sustainability, with the obvious pleasure each generation received from working together.

The role of the middle generation was clearly shown to be in enabling the process to take place. Currently, it is necessary to facilitate a meaningful exchange between the generations which is outside a family relationship. There is also a need for more research that will develop further our understanding of what is taking place in this unique relationship. Intergenerational programmes are an excellent model of citizenship which can be of benefit to us all.

References

Arber, S. and Evandrou, M. (1993) *Ageing, Independence and the Life Course*. London: Jessica Kingsley in association with the British Society.

Bernard, M. (2000) *Promoting Health in Old Age: Critical Issues in Self-health Care*. Buckingham: Open University Press.

Cabinet Office (1991) *The Citizen's Charter: Raising the Standard*, Cm 1599. London: HMSO.

Crewe, I., Searing, D. and Conover, P. (1997) Citizenship: the revival of an idea, in *Citizenship and Civic Education*. London: The Citizenship Foundation.

Davies, S., Elizabeth, S., Hanley, B., New, B. and Sang, B. (1998) *Ordinary Wisdom: Relfections on an Experiment in Citizenship and Health*. London: King's Fund.

Department of Health (1997) *The New NHS: Modern and Dependable*. London: Stationery Office.

Department of Health (1998a) *Our Healthier Nation: A Contract for Health*. London: Stationery Office.

Department of Health (1998b) *Healthy Living Centres: Report of a Seminar*. London: The Department of Health.

Dunning, A. (1999) Stratagem: the better government for older people, *Programme Bulletin*, January: 5–6.

Ellis, S. W. (1998) *The Intergenerational Programme Mentoring Project: Final Research Report*. Stoke-on-Trent: The Beth Johnson Foundation.

Granville, G. (1998) The foundation as a learning organisation, *Education and Ageing*, 13(2): 163–76.

Ivers, V. (1994) *Citizen Advocacy in Action: Working with Older People*. Stoke-on-Trent: The Beth Johnson Foundation in association with the European Commission.

McCrea, J. M. and Smith, T. B. (1997) Types and models in intergenerational programs, in S. Newman, C. R. Ward, T. B. Smith, J. O. Wilson and J. M. McCrea (eds) *Intergenerational Programs – Past, Present and Future*. Washington, DC: Taylor and Francis.

McIver, S. (1998) *Healthy Debate? An Independent Evaluation of Citizens' Juries in Health Settings*. London: King's Fund.

Newman, S. and Marks, S. (1980) *Intergenerational Classroom Teaching Teams: The Effect of Elderly Volunteers, Teachers and Children*. Denver, CO: Association for Gerontology in Higher Education.

Newman, S., Ward, C. R., Smith, T. B., Wilson, J. O. and McCrea, J. M. (eds) (1997) *Intergenerational Programs – Past, Present and Future*. Washington, DC: Taylor & Francis.

Phillipson, C. (1998) *Reconstructing Old Age: New Agendas in Social Theory and Practice*. London: Sage.

Qualifications and Curriculum Authority (1998) *Education for Citizenship and the Teaching of Democracy in Schools: Final Report*. London: QCA Publications.

Social Exclusion Unit (1998) *Bringing Britain Together: A National Strategy for Neighbourhood Renewal*. London: Stationery Office.

4

Lifeskills: from adaptation to transcendence

___ BOB WYCHERLEY _____

Introduction

Life expectancy is rising (Henwood 1992) and the increasing proportion of older people in the population can expect a healthier, more active life. Personality research (e.g. Reichard *et al*. 1962; Neugarten *et al*. 1968; Gaber 1983) suggests different degrees of success in ageing, generally identifying a poorly adjusted group of older people, an adequately adjusted majority with some degree of rigidity and defensiveness and a smaller, exceptionally active, flexible and stable group (e.g. Weeks and James 1998).

This chapter explores skills needed to age successfully, and proposes three levels of these. It deliberately avoids economic issues which may compromise development, reflecting an ideal state of affairs that might only be partially attainable. The justification is the importance of defining ideal ageing in order to know what to aim for. It begins by highlighting the increasing importance of skills as ageing proceeds.

Interactional models of stress

Interactional models of stress (e.g. Cox 1978; Lazarus and Folkman 1984) emphasize our continuous problem-solving in coping with fluctuating demands, and see strain as arising from an imbalance between our perception of demand and our capability. The greater our capability the less susceptible to strain we will be. However, capability is not a unitary category and can be broken down into three elements: internal resources, external resources and skills. Internal resources comprise physical, cognitive and emotional inheritances; for instance, strength, intelligence, emotional stability. External resources are acquired supports, such as money, a confidante or a spiritual framework. Third, skills are practical procedures derived from resources through learning, and examples are arithmetic, driving or managing relationships.

At birth we are virtually without skills, and survive by relying on external resources. The period to young adulthood involves a major shift from dependence on these to reliance on internal resources and skills. Internal resources, in general, peak in early adulthood and gradually decline thereafter (Perlmutter and Hall 1992), though individual variation is considerable, and there is little doubt that the image of ageing as a process of consistent loss is far from the truth (e.g. Cherry and Smith 1998). External resources, on the other hand, may continue to rise as careers progress, stable living situations are established and long-term relationships are made. Skills also continue to develop in occupational, interpersonal, emotional and other areas of life. Age-related decrements in internal resources are thus compensated for by the skills and external resources on which we will increasingly depend as ageing proceeds. Skills are particularly important, both in their own right and as the means of developing external resources.

In the next section some models of adult development are explored to delineate the most basic level of skills which make it possible to cope in later life.

Demand and accommodation

Jung (1930) sees middle age as marked by the re-emergence of the conflict between the person's true nature and the demands of society, which had been resolved by renouncing and denying conflicting wishes, and complying with social expectations. This conflict can be resolved unhealthily by further denial and fanatical clinging to youth, or more healthily by becoming inner-focused and integrating neglected and contradictory aspects of the personality. For Jung this mainly involves acknowledging one's denied characteristics of the opposite sex. This integration can lead to completion of the individual and acceptance of death as part of a larger life process.

Buhler emphasizes striving to reach personal goals and an initial expansion of activities, opportunities and skills (Buhler 1959; Buhler and Massarik 1968; Sugarman 1986). As biological resources decline, activities, ambitions and opportunities shrink, and from middle age past activities are reviewed, setting the scene for the experience of fulfilment, resignation or failure. She emphasizes ongoing attempts to balance equilibrium and change, equilibrium being sought through need satisfaction, and by developing ideals and values giving stability and structure. Change is sought through procreation, work, social contact and other creative operations in the world, though, to achieve this, adaptation and self-restraint are required. In older age a variety of patterns are possible, such as regressive need satisfaction, concern with adaptation to others, enhancement of internal order through life review or continuing creative expansion through the pursuit of existing or new goals.

Erikson (1963, 1980) sees development in terms of a series of crises, arising from social demands, which must be weathered in order to grow. The two final crises are of relevance, the first being generativity versus stagnation. Generativity embraces procreation and an interest in establishing and guiding the next generation, and is not resolved if the individual cannot form intimate relationships or develop a broader caring role in relation to the next generation. The final crisis is ego integrity versus despair and disgust. Successful resolution of preceding crises results in an integrated ego, with acceptance of one's life without excessive regret, one's relatively insignificant place in the universe and other people's expression of their integrity without judgement or threat. If preceding crises are not weathered the result is despair about one's life, and fear of death, as there is no time to alter anything. This may be expressed as disgust with life, particularly with particular institutions or groups.

Havighurst's developmental tasks (Havighurst 1953) are similar to Erikson's crises, though more concrete, and arise from an interaction of physical maturation, cultural expectations and individual aspirations and values. Some examples of middle age tasks are assisting teenage children to become responsible and happy adults, relating to one's spouse as a person and accepting and adjusting to physiological change. Later maturity involves tasks such as adjusting to retirement, reduced income, and the death of one's partner.

Levinson *et al.* (1978) see adult development as evolving through a series of alternating stages of stability and change, each with associated tasks. The later phases of life are concerned with increasing individuation through the resolution of four polarities within the self: attachment/separateness, young/old, destruction/creation and masculine/feminine. Need satisfaction requires accommodation to the outside world, and neglect of our true self, while creative self-development requires inner attention. Grieving for lost youth and relinquishing illusions of immortality can result in a realistic middle age still connected to youthful sources of energy. Mortality can be seen in a context of generational continuity and the 'legacy' a person passes on to future generations. Awareness of mortality brings awareness of destruction and creation as fundamental aspects of life. Guilt about our destructiveness to others, and rage concerning their destructiveness to us, must be faced to affirm life and creativity. We must also come to terms with the elements of the opposite sex in us, making possible new sources of creativeness and more balanced relationships.

For Gould (1978, 1980), adult development involves progressive freedom from childhood rules, standards, irrational assumptions and 'demons' of fear and anger. The developed adult becomes able to live rationally in the real world, a move from 'I am theirs' to 'I own myself'. His final assumption – 'There is no evil in me or death in the world. The sinister has been expelled' – embraces subsidiary beliefs concerning freedom, safety, death and our true nature. Physically ageing, parentless and free of children, we may cling to well worn roles, though the feeling of time running out cannot ultimately be escaped. Men may temporarily maintain control by clinging to work, but expression of neglected aspects of the self becomes more pressing, sometimes leading to radical change. Women may free themselves from an archaic version of femininity and take power over their own lives, challenging their relationship with their partner. The assumption that life would be impossible outside one's relationship can lead to an inability to renegotiate it to accommodate growth and change. It may then break down, or persist in a state of chronic hostility and frustration. Paradoxically, the possibility of losing the relationship must be faced in order to reduce coercion and achieve effective negotiation. Shedding false assumptions confronts us with our true nature, and we must accept our own, and others', 'greed, envy competition, vengeance, blame, hatred and despotic control' (Gould 1978).

A number of models relate specifically to older age. Neugarten (1979) emphasizes 'increased interiority' with age, a process of attending to inner stimuli and the satisfaction of personal needs, coupled with withdrawal from external emotional investments. Typical themes of middle adulthood include restructuring time in terms of 'time left', relating to one's children's partners, accepting grandparenthood and care of parents. Old age themes include resolving grief over loss of work, friends and partner, maintaining integrity in terms of what one was rather than what one is, triumphing in survivorship and accepting forthcoming death.

Cumming and Henry (1961) propose that ageing individuals become progressively disengaged from society. Processes underlying this include making way for the young, avoiding intergenerational conflict, coming to terms with one's life and preparing for death. This model has not received much empirical support, and later models (e.g Havighurst *et al.* 1968) stress the importance of maintaining activity. Rosow (1963) emphasizes the continuation of meaningful activities rather than simply keeping busy and other writers have emphasized the complex relationship between satisfaction and the relevance of activity within the person's historical conception of themselves and their habitual social network (e.g. Kelly *et al.* 1986; Jonsson 1993).

Lifton (1979) sees denied thoughts about death intruding into consciousness in middle age, leading to a sense of time running out. If the certainty of death is not faced, this crisis cannot be resolved and stagnation and numbness results. If death is faced the person can continue to live creatively and with humour, and can contribute to life in the knowledge that death is transcended by culture.

Antonovsky and Sagy (1990) developed a model of retirement transition from Erikson's final stages, suggesting four life tasks:

- reorganization of activities in relation to personal goals and societal expectations;
- achieving meaning by reflecting on past accomplishments and disappointments, examining current satisfactions and planning the future;
- attempting to reach a new view of the world as orderly, manageable and meaningful, rather than chaotic, uncontrollable and confusing;
- awareness of rising morbidity and mortality, leading to greater concern with health.

Significant themes in the models outlined are the successful or unsuccessful adaptation to loss, the maintenance of a satisfactory life pattern and sense of self despite this, life review and acceptance of personal death. The underlying adjustment concept gives a somewhat bleak view of older age, but does, nevertheless, imply a basic level of skill required for survival, albeit one which neglects growth. Figure 4.1 abstracts categories of skill at this basic level from the models reviewed.

Life review
Review and acceptance of one's life as lived
Becoming reconciled to, and responsible for, achievements and failures
Constructing a satisfactory life history

Accepting loss and change
Accepting and adjusting to physical changes
Grieving for the loss of youth, relinquishing beliefs of immortality
Accepting loss of former work and role
Children leaving home, divorcing etc.
Reduced income

Developing a sustainable lifestyle
Deciding what can be sustained and reducing aspirations to this level
Disengaging from unsustainable activities and obligations
Satisfying personal needs
Substitute activity
Developing grandparent role
Meeting social expectations

Maintaining self-esteem
Valuing oneself in terms of what one was rather than what one is
Positive caring for oneself
Affiliating with one's age peers as a normative group

Accepting death
Accepting certainty of personal death
Grieving for loss of partner and close others
Concern about the manner of dying rather than death itself
Making practical preparations for death

Figure 4.1   Accommodation skills.

Growth and management

Despite an emphasis on adaptation, some of the models suggest a further level of skill in which an individual's own beliefs, intentions and expertise interact with events to allow active management of these and continuing personal growth. Figure 4.1 therefore also represents a starting point for this section, which considers the person's own role in ageing.

Peck (1975) suggests the following skills for successful ageing:

- valuing wisdom over physical power;
- accepting reduced sexual drive and valuing people non-sexually;
- accepting loss of adult children and those close, and avoiding social impoverishment through flexible relationships with people of all ages;
- openness to new ways of structuring experience rather than sticking to past rules;
- valuing oneself through a variety of attributes rather than previous roles;

- accepting physical vulnerability and avoiding defining satisfaction in physical terms;
- appreciating one's contribution to the future rather than preoccupation with death.

Pollack (1981) suggests that relinquishing unfulfilled hopes, and mourning the loss of former aspects of the self, frees one from the past, allowing reality to be faced, new investments made and motivation and creativity released.

Baltes and Baltes (1990) point out that many of the decrements of age are due to accumulating pathological incidents and that increasing compression of pathology into a brief period at the end of life (Fries 1990) may result in optimal ageing. They emphasize the considerable reserve capacities of older people, which, though reduced, remain adequate unless demands are extreme. Most older people are capable of learning new skills and achieving excellence, and technology can enhance capability. Successful ageing is facilitated by:

- a healthy, pathology-reducing lifestyle;
- prioritizing to make best use of capacity, motivation and skills;
- establishing realistic goals without loss of selfhood;
- continuously augmenting skills and resources to maintain reserves;
- maintaining personal and societal flexibility;
- use of technical supports and compensatory strategies;
- 'age-friendly' environments which do not exceed reserve capacity and provide enhancing opportunities.

Cognitively, the development of one or more stages beyond Piagetian formal operations has been suggested. Featherman *et al.* (1990) distinguish rational problem-solving and reflective planning, the first requiring technical expertise and the assumption of a best solution, the second a broader, more relative view that there may be a number of solutions with different merits. Reflective planning may be associated with successful ageing by enhancing coping with the ill-defined tasks facing the older person, and is similar to the conception of wisdom of Baltes and Smith (1990), which comprises:

- extensive knowledge of life matters;
- procedures for using this for decision-making and action planning;
- understanding the multiple contexts of life events, their relative importance, interaction and balance;
- knowledge of different human values, goals and priorities, allowing flexible interpretation of events;
- acceptance of risk, allowing decision-making on the basis of probability rather than certainty.

Coleman (1996) points to the importance of self-esteem in successful ageing, and its maintenance through the construction of a satisfactory life story giving meaning, value and control, and by a positive view of ageing. Some older people may achieve a transcendence of self and a wider sense of their place in the universe, particularly in the context of important value systems.

The successful ageing strategies of a 70-year-old man are elucidated by

Sherrard (1998). Her analysis revealed cognitive strategies of reinterpreting age-related changes within a more positive framework and of distancing himself from the unchangeable. Brandtsädter and Baltes-Götz (1990) also suggest a shift in later life from actively changing situations to realistically reducing aspirations to the achievable, allowing maintenance of beliefs of personal control and fostering feelings of well-being and optimism.

The developmental models of Allport (1961) and Maslow (1968, 1970) emphasize internal motivation for personal growth rather than external demands, and imply personal control over one's developmental path. Their conception of the mature adult embraces factors such as self-acceptance, realism, democracy, humour, intimacy and enjoyment of life's basic experiences, coupled with personally developed values which allow transcendence of prevailing cultural pressures and an individually creative approach to life.

This section and parts of the preceding one have introduced a stronger emphasis on continuing personal growth, renegotiation of life contracts and management of resources, which suggest a level of skill above that of basic accommodation. Groups of skills which appear to be required at this level are outlined in Figure 4.2.

Transcendence in older age

The question remains whether, particularly given longer and healthier lives, there may be a further level of skill which will enhance ageing. Older age is a period of profound existential challenge in which former roles defining personhood are removed, strengths diminished and people on whom one depended lost. At the same time one becomes freer of social obligations and open to new possibilities. A key element of chaos theory is the ability of complex adaptive systems to reorganize periodically at a higher level in the face of environmental perturbations (Masterpasqua 1997), and some of the models considered in the last section hint at a higher level of skill which integrates and goes beyond those already considered.

The term 'transcendence' is used for this hypothetical higher level of organization, and groups of 'transcendental skills' are suggested in Figure 4.3. These are not necessarily new, many being hinted at, or explicitly stated, in other work on ageing. However, it is suggested that they can be drawn together to describe what may be the highest level of development in older age, and one which could be increasingly attainable by long-lived adults. That is not to say that all elements will be achieved by any individual and the description represents an ultimate goal rather than an average state.

Transcendence is not intended to imply any mystical quality, though it may include this. It is used in the sense of having come to terms with, and learned to manage, issues such as the body, death or self to a degree where they no longer present problems, and therefore do not require any significant degree of preoccupation. The person, at least most of the time, can be concerned with other, task-related issues, and live beyond his or her body, mortality or ego, a state more unconcerned than mystical.

Transcendental skills present a number of problems. First, they are difficult to define precisely and it is unclear how far separate skills can be identified.

Exploring the interior
Attending to inner world, decreasing dependence on outside world
Reflecting on past accomplishments and failures; restructuring previous experience
as a meaningful basis for proceeding
Reaching a new view of the world as orderly and manageable
Becoming aware of unmet needs and goals
Exploring and developing contradictory and neglected elements of self
Coming to terms with one's negative elements; realistically accepting
one's true nature
Becoming more completely one's true self

Developing autonomous self
Valuing oneself in terms of a variety of attributes rather than previous roles
Developing a positive view of ageing; resisting ageism
Articulating individual value system and living by it, while acknowledging convention
Accepting oneself realistically with humour and tolerance
Becoming autonomous, self-sufficient and responsible for oneself
Accepting aloneness
Becoming natural, spontaneous and creative

Renegotiating relationships
Taking advantage of decreased social prescriptions to become personally and
socially more flexible
Reassessing social and other obligations
Renegotiation of relationship with parents, partner and children
Relating to children as adults, and to their partners
Avoiding social impoverishment by developing flexible relationships with
people of all ages
Tolerance of the differing views and actions of others
Compassionate, democratic concern, empathy and respect for others

Resource management
Reconstruing time as 'time left' and using this as a motivational spur
Relinquishing unattainable goals, and mourning their loss, to free abilities for
future development
Deciding realistic, achievable goals and accepting oneself within this framework
Focusing on high-priority goals
Playing to one's strengths
Treating the practical realities of age as problems to be managed,
not defining characteristics
Reinterpreting the changes of age positively; distancing oneself from
the unchangeable
Learning to pace oneself
Using compensatory technical supports and strategies
Developing a healthy lifestyle to minimize pathology

Developing skills and resources
Enhancing reserve capacity by developing skills and resources
Using community resources for development
Willingness to learn from anybody
Openness to new ways of structuring experience rather than relying on past rules
Consideration of a variety of strategies and solutions for dealing with problems
Trying new solutions and tolerating risk
Realistic perception of events and others

Figure 4.2   Growth and management skills.

Transcending age
Resisting definition by expectations of what is age-appropriate
Being truly oneself regardless of age
Getting on with what one is capable of
Confronting internal 'ageist' beliefs
Valuing the additional skills knowledge and experience of age rather than age itself

Transcending the physical
Managing physical limitations as problems rather than manifestations of deterioration
Rejecting definition of self, or life-satisfaction, in physical terms
Modifying goals in the light of physical limitations but continuing their pursuit
Continuing to enjoy life's physical pleasures
Becoming unbound by gender
Valuing people as individuals and companions more than sexual objects

Transcending time
Focusing on the present quality of experience, valuing process as much as outcome
Continuing commitment to tasks which may never be completed
Living in the present not the past
Appreciating one's life as part of a broader cycle of human history
Developing a philosophy of life which makes time irrelevant

Transcending death
Imposing one's own meaning on life
Developing a sense of one's place in the universe
Seeing one's life as having been meaningfully lived
Appreciating one's contribution to the future rather than preoccupation with
personal death
Assisting the new generation
Appreciating the lives of those lost as part of a broader biological and
cultural process

Transcending relationships
Accepting the fundamental aloneness of all adults
Being alone without concern
Becoming undefined by others, autonomous and independent
Appreciating people as they are rather than by judging them
Relating flexibly to people of all ages

Transcending society
Living by one's internal values
Having values which encompass all humans
Identifying with the human race rather than one's own society
Valuing people above ideology
Valuing people equally
Accepting that there is no fundamentally correct social system

Transcending self
Losing consciousness of self
Being task-centred rather than ego-centred
Losing oneself in tasks and experiences
Becoming creatively guided by one's unconscious processes
Becoming natural and playful

Figure 4.3   Hypothetical transcendental skills.

Second, it is unclear whether they could develop in a partial way; for instance, solely in the physical domain. Finally, there is little research, though with greater longevity there will be increasing opportunities to explore such developmental processes and their relationship to age.

Implications for health promotion

Three levels of living skills have been suggested and these have been called, from less to more complex, accommodation, growth and management, and transcendence. It has been assumed that the higher the level of skill, the more successful ageing will be. Health promotional initiatives directed at the development or enhancement of such skills face a complex task, four components of which are specificity, technique, intervention level and model.

The skills listed in Figures 4.1–4.3 are very general and probably embrace networks of subsidiary skills which will need to be analysed if effective interventions are to be planned. Such analysis is likely to reveal a blend of skills from previous life stages, those specific to older age and those specific to each skill level. At the accommodation level skills such as grieving, developing alternative activities or learning to compare oneself with one's own age group might be important. At the growth and management level, skills such as introspection, tolerance of ambiguity or reflective planning might be of significance. Transcendental skills are more difficult to define but could, for instance, embrace the imposition of personal meaning on life, or enjoying being alone.

This type of analysis also implies the availability of a variety of techniques for facilitating the development of identified skills, some of which, particularly at higher levels of skill, may require a good deal of creativity. These may range across approaches such as personally directed learning, dissemination of information on successful ageing, modification of ageist beliefs, promotion of age-friendly environments, self-development groups or political lobbying for better pensions. Health promotion interventions may be also made at a number of levels of generality – individual, couple/family, group, organization, community and society – and these will require different models and strategies for intervention: behavioural, motivational, attitudinal and political to pinpoint but a few.

An imaginary matrix of skills, versus techniques, versus intervention levels versus models of intervention indicates the complexity of the task facing health promotion with older people. This, coupled with lack of knowledge of the development of older people who are healthier and longer lived than ever before, the pace of technological change and demographic changes making the contribution of older people to the workforce more critical, sets a formidable agenda for health promotion in the twenty-first century.

References

Allport, G. W. (1961) *Pattern and Growth in Personality*. New York: Holt, Rinehart and Winston.

Antonovsky, A. and Sagy, S. (1990) Confronting developmental tasks in the retirement transition, *The Gerontologist*, 30(3): 362–8.

Baltes, P. B and Baltes, M. M (1990) Psychological perspectives on successful aging: the model of selective optimisation with compensation, in P. B. Baltes and M. M. Baltes (eds) *Successful Aging: Perspectives from the Behavioral Sciences*. New York: Cambridge University Press.

Baltes, P. B. and Smith, J. (1990) Toward a psychology of wisdom and its ontogenesis, in R. J. Sternbeg (ed.) *Wisdom: Its Nature, Origins, and Development*. New York: Cambridge University Press.

Brandtsädter, J. and Baltes-Götz, B. (1990) Personal control over development and quality of life perspectives in adulthood, in P. Baltes and M. Baltes (eds) *Successful Aging: Perspectives from the Behavioral Sciences*. Cambridge: Cambridge University Press.

Buhler, C. (1959) Theoretical observations about life's basic tendencies, *American Journal of Psychotherapy*, 13(3): 561–81.

Buhler, C. and Massarik, F. (eds) (1968) *The Course of Human Life: A Study of Goals in the Humanistic Perspective*. New York: Springer.

Cherry, K. E. and Smith, A. D. (1998) Normal memory aging, in M. Hersen and V. B. van Hasselt (eds) *Handbook of Clinical Geropsychology*. New York: Plenum Press.

Coleman, P. G. (1996) Identity management in later life, in R. T. Woods (ed.) *Handbook of the Clinical Psychology of Ageing*. Chichester: Wiley.

Cox, T. (1978) *Stress*. London: The Macmillan Press.

Cumming, E. and Henry, W. H. (1961) *Growing Old: The Process of Disengagement*. New York: Basic Books.

Erikson, E. H. (1963) *Childhood and Society*, rev. edn. New York: W. W. Norton.

Erikson, E. H. (1980) *Identity and the Life Cycle*. New York: W. W. Norton.

Featherman, D. L., Smith, J. and Peterson, J. G. (1990) Successful ageing in a post-retired society, in P. Baltes and M. Baltes (eds) *Successful Aging: Perspectives from the Behavioral Sciences*. Cambridge: Cambridge University Press.

Fries, J. F. (1990) Medical perspectives upon successful aging, in P. Baltes and M. Baltes (eds) *Successful Aging: Perspectives from the Behavioral Sciences*. Cambridge: Cambridge University Press.

Gaber, L. B. (1983) Activity/disengagement revisited: personality types in the aged, *British Journal of Psychiatry*, 143: 490–7.

Gould, R. L. (1978) *Transformations: Growth and Change in Adult Life*. New York: Simon & Schuster.

Gould, R. L. (1980) Transformational tasks in adulthood, in S. I. Greenspan and G. H. Pollock (eds) *The Course of Life: Psychoanalytic Contributions toward Understanding Personality Development, Volume 3: Adulthood and the Aging Process*. Washington, DC: National Institute for Mental Health.

Havighurst, R. J. (1953) *Human Development and Education*. New York: Longman.

Havighurst, R. J., Neugarten, B. L. and Tobin, S. (1968) Disengagement and patterns of aging, in B. I. Neugarten (ed.) *Middle Age and Aging: A Reader in Social Psychology*. Chicago: University of Chicago Press.

Henwood, M. (1992) *Through a Glass Darkly: Community Care and Elderly People*. Research report no. 14. London: King's Fund Institute.

Jonsson, H. (1993) The retirement process in an occupational perspective: a review of literature and theories, *Physical and Occupational Therapy in Geriatrics*, 11(4): 15–34.

Jung, C. G. (1930) The stages of life, in C. S. Jung, *The Collected Works, Volume 8*. New York: Pantheon.

Kelly, J. R., Steincamp, M. W. and Kelly, J. R. (1986) Later life leisure: how they play in Peoria, *The Gerontologist*, 26(5): 531–7.

Lazarus, R. S. and Folkman, S. (1984) *Stress, Appraisal and Coping*. New York: Springer.

Levinson, D. J., Darrow, D. N., Klein, E. B., Levinson, M. H. and McKee, B. (1978) *The Seasons of a Man's Life*. New York: A. A. Knopf.

Lifton, R. J. (1979) *The Broken Connection*. New York: Simon & Schuster.

Maslow, A. H. (1968) *Toward a Psychology of Being*. New York: Van Nostrand Reinhold.

Maslow, A. H. (1970) *Motivation and Personality*. New York: Harper & Row.

Masterpasqua, F. (1997) Toward a dynamical developmental understanding of disorder, in F. Masterpasqua and P. A. Perna (eds) *The Psychological Meaning of Chaos*. Washington, DC: American Psychological Association.

Neugarten, B. L. (1979) Time, age and the life cycle, *American Journal of Psychiatry*, 136(7): 887–94.

Neugarten, B. L., Havighurst, R. J., and Tobin, S. S. (1968) Personality and patterns of ageing, in B. L. Neugarten (ed.) *Middle Age and Ageing*. Chicago: University of Chicago Press.

Peck, R. (1975) Psychological development in the second half of life, in W. C. Sze (ed.) *Human Life Cycle*. New York: Jason Aronson Inc.

Perlmutter, M. and Hall, E. (1992) *Adult Development and Aging*. New York: Wiley.

Pollack, G. H. (1981) Aging or aged: development or pathology, in S. I. Greenspan and G. H. Pollack (eds) *The Course of Life: Psychoanalytic Contributions toward Understanding Personality Development, Volume 3: Adulthood and the Ageing Process*. Washington, DC: National Institute of Mental Health.

Reichard, S., Livson, F., and Peterson, P. G. (1962) *Ageing and Personality: A Study of Eighty Seven Older Men*. New York: Wiley.

Rosow, I. (1963) Adjustment of the normal aged, in R. H. Williams, C. Tibbits and W. Donahue (eds) *Processes of Aging, Volume 2*. New York: Atherton.

Sherrard, C. (1998) Strategies for well-being in later life: a qualitative analysis, *British Journal of Medical Psychology*, 71: 253–63.

Sugarman, L. (1986) *Life-span Development: Concepts, Theories and Interventions*. London: Methuen.

Weeks, D. and James, J. (1998) *Superyoung: The Proven Way to Stay Young Forever*. London: Hodder & Stoughton.

5

The ageless self: exploring holism

CAROLINE NASH

If we were asked to think for a while about our 'self' and our health, I wonder what sort of thoughts would go through our minds. Where would we centre our self: in the head, the heart, the body? Would we consider the ego? The ego is seen by many as the 'selfish' self and consequently efforts are made to subdue it. Would we contemplate our self-image or the image we believe others have of us?

Often the self conjures up our personality, but if we talk of the health of the self, body as well as mind becomes involved. When asked to describe health, a large proportion of people of all ages refer to health in bodily terms such as 'fitness', 'ability to perform certain acts' and 'absence of disease'. Interestingly, though, as people age and/or have deficiencies in their bodies, they frequently still consider themselves to be healthy. For instance, a diabetic, a visually impaired person or someone restricted by arthritis may still believe himself or herself to be in a good state of health. Is it possible then that these people, who may objectively lack complete health, have a more 'holistic' view of themselves and of health than do the younger and fitter?

Modern lifestyles bring us up to be analytical and separatist, rather than to synthesize and see things as integral parts of wholes. We divide days up into hours and minutes of set length, although we all know that some days seem to last longer than others. At school and beyond, in libraries and centres of learning, we divide the world into discrete subjects, yet can it really be possible to consider history apart from the geographical environment, the languages spoken and the foods eaten? We all know that wars can be started by mistranslated or misinterpreted messages and won or lost due to weather conditions, harsh terrain and food shortages.

Separation

It should not be surprising that we perceive humans as operating upon the environment rather than being an integral part of it, or that we act as individuals even when we want to consider ourselves as part of a family or wider community.

So, too, we are taught to divide up the self. We are body, mind, emotions and spirit or soul. As far back as Roman times, people were exhorted to have a healthy mind in a healthy body. Today we are encouraged not to let our hearts rule our head. Ascetics throughout the ages have tried to sublimate the body by concentrating on things of the spirit.

The medical profession is renowned for its habit of considering patients as parts rather than whole human beings. Surgeons operate on a specific part of the body, while the rest of it is covered so as not to distract them. Later they review the patient as the 'gall bladder' or 'perforated ulcer', rather than Ms Jones or Mr Smith. Even their symptoms and signs together make up a certain disease pattern or syndrome and thus permit a medical label to be attached to the human being who is suffering the condition.

An individual is also very likely to see himself or herself as many separate (and often conflicting) parts within one being. One part of us happily reaches for yet another chocolate to assuage the appetite's craving, while another part roundly condemns us for succumbing. Somehow most of us find it quite normal to have our minds in turmoil most of the time, struggling with the cognitive dissonance of conflicting thoughts (original concepts developed by Festinger 1957). The gap between attitudes or beliefs and behaviour has long troubled health educators, aware that the former may have little or no influence upon the latter. Almost all smokers must know by now of the ill effects of their habit, yet they continue to pay high prices in order to enjoy a short-term something, which in the long term will probably curtail their life or render their later years unhealthy and uncomfortable.

It may well be that this separateness which we almost all experience is something that we are taught, rather than something that comes naturally to us. Babies and young children seem able just to 'be', following their own nature without self-judgement until adults intervene with their 'you should do this' and 'you mustn't do that'. Adults use these strategies to seek to protect offspring and because of their own inner messages. Not surprisingly, it is not that long before the child begins to internalize the rules and devise his or her own series of musts and shoulds, combined with the usual sense of self-blame and unworthiness when the rules are broken.

The need to enable children to grow safely within appropriate boundaries requires parents or caring guardians, who are often hard pressed, to distinguish an inappropriate action of the child from the child itself. So it is not 'Naughty Simon or Sue', but 'Don't tip your food on the floor, and keep your food on the table.' The second statement distinguishes the action or behaviour of the child, from the child itself. The same process can be applied to the expression of emotions by an individual. When a child is crying the child can be acknowledged and the feeling expressed identified as being of the child, but not the same as the whole child him or herself. So the comment 'You are always crying' (which obviously cannot be true, though that is the way it may feel to a beleaguered, desperate and exhausted parent) could beneficially be replaced by 'You seem sad, are you (. . . in pain, . . . frustrated, . . . hurting etc.). Thus the necessary acknowledgement and the necessary caring can be provided.

As our bodies age and alter, it is a truism that we ourselves do not necessarily feel that the 'inside' keeps pace with the 'outside' (Featherstone and Hepworth 1989). Hence the slender person peeps out from the fat person's body and may buy clothes sizes too small, not just because there is a hope that diets may achieve the slimming miracle, but also because the person inside used to wear a size 10 and in part cannot believe that the change has occurred. Within the imagination those clothes will fit. Likewise, the 80-year-old 'wrinkly' still may feel 18 years old inside and may be shocked when the ageing body does not respond as it once did. The young mind is trapped and therefore feels separate from the old body, just as the thin body is trapped within the fat one.

Holism

It seems to me that what is needed in order to be whole is 'everything'. For too long we have denied the softer, more feminine and intuitive parts of ourselves in favour of the more acquisitive, aggressive, masculine side. However, almost as a reflex reaction we are now in danger of swinging too far and too fast in the opposite direction. It would indeed be rash to discard such essential creativity. Technology has provided the potential for us to communicate instantly at a vast distance and to be able to provide everyone with enough food and clean water. Returning to days of subsistence farming would not be desirable for most of us, though the idea of doing some organic gardening may be attractive.

So in what ways can we become integrated? What can help us to feel whole? Does it mean that we have to be able to do everything ourselves? As a reaction against specialization into absurdity, must we now all become jacks of all trades and masters of none? To contemplate this is to put an even greater burden on ourselves.

If no one trains to become a specialist car mechanic or plumber, must we attempt to do everything ourselves and not be permitted to use mechanized things unless we understand them enough to correct them if they go wrong? When a gadget or my car misbehaves I experience enormous relief when I know it will be returned to me later, in good working order, with nothing required of myself in exchange other than money. Likewise, I don't expect my patients to have a detailed knowledge of the inner workings of their bodies or the curative properties of homeopathic medicines. That is my expertise.

To be whole does not mean to be everything. Holism instead means not denying parts of ourselves, taking everything into account as far as possible.

Holism is not only an individual thing. We are whole as parts of a 'larger' whole. Indeed, it is essential to perceive of ourselves as a part of our environment. If we see ourselves as individuals with our own tasks to perform within an overall organism, which requires each and every one of us, in order to complete and to function properly, we at once become small, with our own specific task to perform, and also hugely important to everyone and every-thing else.

In this way the milkman has a vital function in communicating between animal, farmer and producer and the consumer who needs to be fed before performing his or her equally vital task. We are all necessary, but different rather than separate, just like different parts of the body. Some may have a purely decorative function, but who will tell us that this is unimportant? The hair, for instance, is our crowning glory and, though a woolly hat would do as well to keep us warm, we all know how important hair (and hence our hairdressers) is to how we feel about ourselves.

Holistic therapies attempt to see and treat the body as a whole, taking full account of body, mind and spirit. What we seem to need are therapists who will walk alongside us to help us to integrate the different parts of ourselves, converging all the separated parts and denying none, even those hidden from view from patients themselves. And we need to accept that we are all patients in that we are all seekers, if not of *the* truth (whatever that may be) then of *our own* truth. Just as we all are patients/seekers, so anyone and anything can be our therapist and help us along our path to healing. A beautiful sunset or a spreading oak tree may achieve as much good or positive change as five years of counselling or herbs. And both may be needed.

Healing, then, or so it seems to me, is an integration of all parts rather than a disparate separateness: an acceptance of all that we have and all that we are, and also a recognition and acceptance of what we are not. Such an integration will bring about peace within, for then the constant seeking and constant comparing of ourselves with others will cease. And enlightenment is inner peace, which allows inner light; peace inside, in that part which does not and has not ever aged: an acknowledgement of that part which is, indeed, our spirit, the same spirit which is within us all and can never die; a spirit which is part of the whole spirit.

Integration

Nowadays the West will often look towards Eastern traditions and cultures for clues as to how to become more integrated or 'at one', believing that these ancient cultures are more in tune with their environment and more 'whole' than we are. Is this really the case? In both China and India, the homes of successful forms of traditional medicines and spiritual beliefs, skyscrapers are springing up ever quicker and the younger generations are eager to speak English and wear Western designer clothes. If we look at older generations and communities which live outside the larger rapidly developing cities, we certainly find traditional values still. However, in many cases, when we look more closely at these, they too often separate the human being, even in their attempts to be spiritual.

In meditation, we are told to still the mind and forget the bodily needs while focusing on 'higher' things. Indeed, some teachers are harsh disciplinarians and will use a stick to make sure their pupils are sitting correctly. There is not much natural flow there. Hindus also have a tendency to categorize and separate. The caste system is not integrating. If we consider an individual rather than society at large, we also find a lot of 'shoulds'. A man has a series of tasks to perform: to obey parents and learn; then to give back by working and bringing up a family; with that achieved he should then develop his spiritual side and withdraw from day-to-day society. Everything is there, but as a series of steps rather than as an integrated whole.

Perhaps we are expecting too much of ourselves. Perhaps integration really is a step ladder. Certainly the Hindu idea is similar to Maslow's pyramid of needs which lead to self-actualization. Surely, it is self-evident that for most people it would be impossible to concentrate the mind very effectively on beauty and God if they were cold and hungry.

Yet many examples of enlightenment seem to have occurred precisely when someone was starving and freezing to death. Victor Frankl's search for meaning in life took place amidst the Nazi death camps, and it was within that most awful of contexts that he was able to transcend the daily grind, and even help others to find a reason for life (Frankl 1997). Perhaps somewhat strangely to us today, in the past people sought out similar difficult living situations. Saints and ascetics throughout the ages and in all cultures have deliberately deprived the body in order to bring about a sense of something beyond the everyday self. Simon the Stylite spent years on top of a pole in Syria. In India fakirs lie on beds of nails and in North America and Africa people have gone off alone to fast in the wilderness (just as Christ did) to seek out understanding.

Such means of depriving the body in some way is in order to heighten spiritual awareness are being practised more and more today by New Age followers. Examples are fire-walking, in which participants walk barefoot over glowing hot coals, and vision quests, in which people go to a sacred place and stay awake for 24 hours or more without food in the hope that some inner knowledge will come to them in the form of a vision or daydream.

Obviously, nowadays many people of all ages are seeking out meaning and a way of life which does not perceive them to be purely physical bodies that need to be fed and kept fit simply in order to be able to produce more, in terms of ideas and ultimately money; nor even, following Darwin, as organisms apparently with the sole purpose of reproduction and taking over more and more of the Earth as the dominant species.

Older people as examples of whole beings

In our later years we have the potential to develop into the most 'whole' people within our communities. Just by dint of age, older people are bound to have experienced more than younger members of society. Within the family they will certainly know what it is like to be a child and have little power, have probably also experienced the responsibilities and commitment of being a spouse and parent, and may currently be taking on the role of grandparent. Their lives may have included divorce and bereavement. Within society they will have been a pupil and possibly a teacher or carer of some kind. They will probably have worked in various places and done several jobs, and some will have experienced periods of unemployment and redundancy.

With all this wealth of experience, older people must have felt a gamut of emotions, including joy, grief, fear, hope, sadness, disillusionment and anger. How can older people fail to have acquired within themselves some degree of wisdom? Unless we suffer from some form of memory loss, each new experience builds on the last, it does not replace it. Research shows that the brain can store far more information than we ask it to. So older people will still know what it is to laugh and play as a child while the freedom which comes with lessening responsibility and decreasing concern for the good opinion of others. Older people are often ready to be themselves and dress exactly as they please (which often means merely comfortably), which is often termed the 'second childhood'.

Being whole is perhaps the aim of being human. This means knowing and being old and young at the same time, having awareness of the possible consequences of our actions and deciding whether or not to go ahead anyway.

Cultures which have, perhaps, respected their elders more than the West does today are often held up as being shining examples of how we should treat our own older generations. Certainly it makes sense to use the wisdom gathered over the years, but we need to take care that this does not place the older person in some sort of straitjacket, so that to gain respect and retain a position in the community the older person loses his or her individual identity and becomes a 'role', as can occur in Eastern households, where the mother-in-law exerts influence over the daughter-in-law because of what she is and can lose her inner self in the process.

Biological age and perceived age

There has been a slogan in a shoe shop chain recently which exhorts us to 'act our shoe size' rather than our age. What a wonderful idea this seems. If we use British sizing no one will be older than 13, although I'm not sure how many of us would enjoy being incontinent, dribbling one-year-olds needing to be spoon fed! In continental sizing the maximum age would be around 50, and some younger people might find themselves expected to wear sober suits. None the less, the concept behind the slogan – that we should all loosen up and dance and skip – certainly has an appeal.

There is evidence that stress and responsibility can make an individual grow up and grow older before the norm. Likewise, those who look young for their years frequently act and feel so. Encouraging people to remain as active and healthy as possible throughout life is a major aim of health promotion and, no doubt, of all of us. From time to time campaigns have been run by the Health Education Authority with the specific objective of raising older people's awareness of health issues and providing them with ideas and information on how to stay well. During the 1980s and 1990s AgeWell, in collaboration with Age Concern England, 50 Plus, All to Play For, the Sports Council, local health promotion teams, Age Concern groups and sports centres, has taken up the idea, in some areas, of running special classes and groups for retired people interested in helping themselves to keep well, sometimes with GP referral.

Whatever the course or system is called, it will almost invariably include the areas of mental health, physical fitness, environment, nutrition and social interaction. Being at ease in all these areas will almost certainly increase the happiness and decrease the level of ill-health not just in older people, but in anyone, no matter what age they may be. So we all benefit from:

- having interests and hobbies which take us out of ourselves (mental health);
- opportunities for enjoyment, pleasure, fun, release of tension (mental health);
- keeping ourselves flexible and taking exercise (physical health);
- living in a warm dry home with clean air and pleasant surroundings (environmental health and mental health);
- eating fresh, nutritious, varied and well cooked food (physical and dietary health);
- having friends and/or family to make us feel loved and needed (social health).

With all of the above in place an individual is well placed to take his or her focus away from his or her apparent self, away from the (usually younger adult) preoccupation with looks and image, out of consideration of others, which develops the social self, and to contemplation of matters of the ultimate meaning of life (whether within the structure of organized religion or not), which develops the spiritual self. The development of these two 'selves' is surely without reference to age and allows us to find our true selves, often within a 'oneness' or identification with all our fellow beings. Only then, perhaps, can we find ourselves at the same time. Paradoxically, we lose our self and thus become whole.

Conclusion

The 'ageless self' refers to the integral parts of a person which do not appear to age chronologically. The rate of physical ageing is complex and dependent on many internal and external factors. Health promotion depends on professionals recognizing the variety of routes into older age. The many needs that older people may have in relation to their identity and recognition correspond to the underlying pattern of being. The holistic nature – the spiritual self integrated within the whole – is ageless, infinite and transcendent. This has implications for ongoing spiritual development and maturity, life planning, life and death education and ways to achieve a fulfilled life. In the development of the spiritual aspect some of the other aspects of the whole person will be supported, including emotional, mental, physical and social. This will include creating a supportive environment in which the individual can function as a whole, by relating the whole person's needs to his or her environment.

References

Berne, E. (1964) *The Games People Play*. New York: Grove Press.
Burns, R. B. (1979) *The Self Concept: Theory, Measurement and Behaviour*. London: Longman.

Carter, T. and Nash, C. (1993) *AgeWell Planning and Ideas Pack*, 3rd edn. London: Age Concern England.

Coni, N., Davison, W. and Webster, S. (1986) *Ageing: The Facts*. Oxford: Oxford Medical Publications.

Featherstone, M. and Hepworth, M. (1989) Ageing and old age: reflections on the postmodern life course, in B. Bytheway, T. Keil, P. Allat and A. Bryman (eds) *Becoming and Being Old: Sociological Approaches to Later Life*. London: Sage.

Festinger, L. (1957) *The Theory of Cognitive Dissonance*. Evanston, IL: RUW Peterson.

Frankl, V. E. (1997) *Man's Search for Ultimate Meaning*. New York: Insight Books.

Ginn, J., Arber, S. and Cooper, H. (1997) *Researching Older People's Health Needs and Health Promotion Issues*. London: Health Education Authority.

Kaufman, S. R. (1986) *The Ageless Self: Sources of Meaning in Late Life*. Madison: University of Wisconsin Press.

Killoran, A., Howse, K. and Dalley, G. (eds) (1997) *Promoting the Health of Older People: A Compendium*. London: Health Education Authority.

Maslow, A. H. (1954) *Motivation and Personality*. New York: Harper.

Nash, C. and Carter, T. (1992) *The AgeWell Handbook: Setting up Community Health Initiatives with Older People*. London: Age Concern England.

Nash, C. L. (1998) *Consider the Alternatives: Healthy Strategies for Later Life*. London: Third Age Press.

Victor, C. (1987) *Old Age in Modern Society*. London: Croom Helm.

PART 2

Practical issues in health promotion with older people

This second part of the book focuses on particular issues which can be a concern to older people and health professionals to whom they relate. The order of the chapters is somewhat arbitrary. They are potentially all useful and informative.

The issues of paid work and productivity are tackled by Joanna Walker. This area is of concern, since paid work has been identified as contributing significantly to self-identity and sense of worth. Mary Davies tackles the area of sexual activity and ageing and encourages the professional to take a non-ageist and non-moralist view of sexual activity among older people. This is followed by Alison Allen's description of an innovative fall prevention approach which is comprehensive and detailed. The chapter describes ongoing research in a primary care setting.

At no age are people without some kind of loss, and therefore grief. Patricia Hayman and Nerys James capture the essential and necessary role of the health and social worker in enabling the grief experience for older people, demonstrating that the professionals' own personal dilemmas with respect to grief interfere with their ability to work successfully with others.

The next two chapters consider particular issues facing older people. Anne Squire reviews health promotion within a residential setting and provides insightful ways in which activities can be designed by residential home organizers and staff. Finally, Stephen Clift and Matthew Morrissey cover an area of increasing importance for all ages, especially older people – travel health.

6

Health and productive ageing

___ JOANNA WALKER ___

Most modern societies place a high value on work. It may be unequally shared, with some individuals and groups doing more than others, or work of different kinds, but the work ethic remains a potent political and social force. Commentators on the sociology of work and how it is defined, managed, distributed and rewarded make much of the historical changes associated with the coming of 'modernity'. Prior to this, older civilizations (Greek, Roman or Hebrew, for example) had regarded work as a low-status activity, fit for slaves, or as punishment or duty to be endured; downgrading, not ennobling. One's citizenship and participation in society were related to other activities and statuses, not to work or occupation. Leisure and enjoyment were higher callings, to which ends work could be tolerated.

The value of work

Our modern esteem of work and purposive occupation is seen as deriving from Reformation values (the so-called Protestant work ethic) which enabled personal effort and devotion to become the means of reward and status, both human and divine (Harris 1990). The fullest expression of this value is, perhaps, associated with the period of industrialization experienced by Western nations in the eighteenth and nineteenth centuries. Work became additional to and separated from that which took place in the home, and regulated by external agencies and forces. Labour and its reproduction drove the new engines of society.

If industrialization represented the supremacy of the machine over the body, the post-industrial age has been described as the supremacy of the mind over the body (Osgood 1982). Acquiring and applying knowledge are mental labours that increased their dominance throughout the twentieth century, emphasizing a work ethic driven by self-enhancement and self-expression.

We have bought into work as both a means (e.g. to material goods) and an end in itself (e.g. as self-actualization). However, we still define leisure as non-work, whereas the Greeks defined work as non-leisure.

In the developed post-industrialized economies, then, work in the broadest sense (including paid and unpaid, formal and informal roles that are purposive and other-directed) has become a dominant value and mechanism for social engagement. In the 1950s, the emerging discipline of sociology identified five general functions that work performed in the life of individuals. These were: financial return in exchange for labour; regulation of life activity (when, where and how people spend time); creation of a sense of identity and status; provision of a base for social relations; opportunity of meaningful life experiences (interaction, ideas, challenges) (Friedmann and Havighurst 1954).

While these functions of work are expressed in very general terms, they do enable the useful observation that none of them is age-related. The fact that we do not tend to link older age with work is to do with the history of how work came to be distributed during the twentieth century, not because of the nature of either later life or work. With the growth of welfare systems, certain categories of exemption from the obligation to work began to be defined and operationalized. Age exemptions by virtue of youth or old age were among the most obvious. Subsequently, other major grounds for exemption have been health- and disability-related. Less directly, the importance to society of roles incompatible with employment has also been recognized (e.g. parenting, care-giving). Arguably, the latter represent alternative forms of work, on a broader definition.

We have become aware of the provisional nature of these exemptions since the 1980s, as the trends in all mature welfare states have been to review and reduce them. Thus the state pension eligibility age for women increases, disabled people and single parents face more stringent tests for state support, students take loans rather than receive grants etc. There is talk in the media about a demographic timebomb reducing our ability to support pensions systems. The ageing of both developed and developing nations is indeed a significant factor, but a society's age structure is one variable among many for policy decision-making, not a problem in itself.

There are two social trends that are currently influencing the ways in which variables such as age, health and work are being seen as interrelated. These are the *changes taking place in the social institution of retirement*, and the recognition of the *shift to a postmodern phase of society with its inherent danger of social exclusion*. The next section of this chapter refers to these two trends as frameworks through which to examine the notion that health is related to work and purposive activity. It is argued that health always was and will again become a key factor in older people's ability and obligation to be seen as 'productive'.

Retirement: a twentieth-century achievement

The transformation of retirement from elite privilege to mass experience, mostly within fifty years, is truly an achievement of modern welfare societies.

Retirement, along with shorter working hours and paid holidays, has been instrumental in reducing the proportion of people's lives spent doing work. Before retirement became the expectation of the majority, made increasingly possible by pensions, the only exit route from work was ill-health and infirmity. Now, although ill-health and disability still form significant routes to retirement for some (Laczko and Phillipson 1991), these are no longer required as justifications for retirement *per se*, which has established itself as a legitimate status for its occupants, and an accepted part of the lifecourse.

Although retirement, throughout its hundred year development, has been conceptualized in a number of ways (Walker 1996), there are some prevailing concepts or models of retirement that are particularly relevant to the relationship between health and productivity in later life. First, as we have seen, retirement is by definition non-productive, and represents one's permission to leave the labour market, or one's exclusion from it, depending on economic conditions. In this sense it represents sanctioned unemployment (Montgomery *et al*. 1990). It is a change of status and in relationship to society (pensioner rather than producer), and is discontinuous with the past. Alternatively, it is a reward for past productivity, supported by savings (deferred wages) in the form of pensions (Ekerdt 1986).

Phillipson and Walker and others have made a case that, although accepted as a non-productive status, retirement has at various periods been encouraged or discouraged by both formal and informal policy measures, according to prevailing economic and, in particular, labour market conditions. It is also suggested that gerontology and geriatric medicine research has in these various periods investigated the health effects of continuing to work (delaying retirement to retain the benefits of work) *and* of entering retirement (to gain health benefits of not working or avoid health costs of work), according to prevailing philosophy.

Another influential view of retirement as a different, discontinuous state or stage has been the notion of a 'third age', characterized by self-fulfilment. In its original formulation (Laslett 1989), the third age lifestyle did not exclude work, as long as it was fulfilling, leading to greater self-actualization. The presumption was that such experiences were more likely to be found in activities which were not primarily for productive purposes. The potential health benefits were all those that could be seen as arising from a release from non self-actualizing activity and control by external agencies to a self-directed state that could address psychological, social, emotional, even spiritual needs.

The third age as a lifestyle option arose, arguably, as a challenge to the potentially passive view of retirement as non-work, which therefore equated it with leisure. It also sought to demonstrate that third agers were not only healthy but could, by their own strivings to fulfil themselves, maintain their health for longer. It challenged the implication that retirement was for weaklings, for those who needed a rest, or who had no further ambitions beyond work. Because third age living was inherently active, it could not be accused of inducing ill-health, as some research had suggested retirement might.

Although proudly active, the 'third age' concept of retirement was essentially non-productive in the sense that the value to the self was the main reason for activity, rather than producing goods or services or enabling others to do so, or adding economic value. The idea of a third age, however, has had a considerable impact on our general understandings of later life, making a dent in a previously almost universally negative image. It has also refocused arguments about health in later life, stressing the role of personal resources and self-image and confidence in one's role as an older person. It has emphasized the health potential of the *constructive*, rather than the *productive*, as the ideal type of activity (Caro *et al*.1993).

We have seen how retirement has become accepted as a non-work status, as earned leisure, supported by efforts made earlier in life, but some authors have observed that since the work ethic is so strong, it is probably quite difficult to extinguish it, even given permission to do so. Ekerdt (1986) has suggested that the work ethic is replaced by the 'busy ethic', which mimics the work ethic to some extent, including the regulation of pseudo-work (busyness) with periods of leisure within retirement. Presumably, there could be health gains through the loss of real work-related stresses, and the assumption of control of one's agenda. However, if busy-ness is evidence of work substitution because its loss is not accepted, this may be less healthy. The health benefits of negotiating the transition to a new stage in life such as retirement have been documented and built into modern pre-retirement education practice (Coleman and Chiva 1992).

It is now clear that a period of 'discouraged' retirement has been entered, as occupational pension schemes can no longer support the levels of early retirement enhancements with which they assisted the downsizing of the late 1980s and 1990s. Taken together with the trend to reduce welfare support and promote self-reliance, the *permission and right to work* established by third agers has moved closer to being a positive *encouragement to work* in later life. Self-fulfilment is being superseded by 'productive ageing', with its inherent challenge to demonstrate continued participation in productive terms. In effect, retirement as leisure or as self-directed development is becoming less tenable unless, of course, adequate funds have been generated to avoid any call on public support. The hint of ambiguity in whether retirement remains a legitimate non-productive status can be seen, for instance, in the debate around the future of the state pension: is it a right, paid for by past productivity (as widely believed), or a transfer payment reliant on continuing support in the present?

On leaving the twentieth century, then, we see the sweep of development of the social institution of retirement, from elite experience to mass expectation and, perhaps, back again (to those who can afford it). The recent success of those who sought to make work a choice in retirement, or to postpone retirement and to stake their claim in the labour market, may have won a battle, but the terms of engagement are changing. They now join those whose pensions have never been adequate for a work-free retirement in a labour market that is ageist, despite some new awareness regarding older workers.

Their problem is that the end of work for many people is now separated by some years from when they, and society, think is an appropriate time for retirement. To negotiate that gap, people in their fifties and sixties must rely on health and opportunity to continue earning. Actual retirement, then, as a phase in which work is seen as inappropriate, will move on to what has been termed the 'fourth age'. By definition this is a time when the capacity to maintain oneself independently begins to reduce, and interdependence with or dependency on others, including the state, is seen as necessary. As this stage will be reached at varying ages, retirement will once again be linked to infirmity rather than a qualifying age or set of entitlements.

The postmodern society, risk and opportunity

In some significant ways, the third age lifestyle movement was essentially postmodern. It challenged normative patterns of behaviour for older people and sought to open up a range of choices for both 'being' and 'doing' in later life. It promoted not only paid work but also unpaid, voluntary and civic roles, participation and social engagement of all kinds *because* all these things could be pursued once one was free of work obligations. With the rise of productive ageing, the support that underpins such activities must come from the individual, who must first see to his or her own maintenance. So constructive activity is fine, especially if it plays a preventive health role, but productive activity is better. A drop in third age volunteering is already noticeable, according to the relevant agencies.

Our post-industrial, postmodern age has been described as a 'risk' society. We are freer to choose and change our path, but the price is constant attention to resources, planning and risk management (Henley Centre, 1998). The changing nature of work, the end of the traditional idea of career, the need for frequent retraining, the lack of continuity of employment and a retreat from corporate welfare make the goal of lifelong earning a difficult one to achieve. Yet our third ages will depend on the provision that earnings translated into pensions can make. Maintaining capacity is clearly going to be a key factor in quality of life, not only for individuals and families, but also for society, if anyone is ever to have any spare resource to invest in the community.

In an attempt to address the obvious potential dangers of increasing individual responsibility, another aspect of current socio-political development is the emphasis on inclusion or, rather, efforts to combat exclusion. With productive ageing no longer a discontinuous state, like retirement, older people are increasingly seen as engaging on the same terms as other adults: producers, consumers, citizens. The drive for inclusion needs to address all aspects of access to productive success, such as training, equal opportunities and support to enable work availability (e.g. affordable care facilities for dependants). In a culture where the value of work remains high, third agers have already demonstrated themselves fit, able and willing.

However, will their willingness remain at a high level if the voluntary nature of productivity begins to reduce? Again, it may depend on the support systems mentioned above, which will tell them that they are valued workers, as well as the treatment of those whose fitness no longer enables participation. As in other periods of discouraged retirement, research and development resources are being invested in exploring the benefits of productive activity. Good health is seen as a key factor, both as a pre-existing condition of continuing work (in the broadest sense) and as an outcome of remaining engaged: both cause and effect of productivity.

Although the risk society may tend to see health maintenance as an individual responsibility, enough is known about the production of ill-health and disability for a mature society to acknowledge that collective action is also necessary. Just as there are benefits to the individual and to the community of staying well and engaged, there are also costs to both parties of maintaining and improving health.

Benefits and costs of investing in health: the role of purposive activity

In this discussion of the literature on the health effects of purposive or productive activity, three main areas are used as a focus: the rehabilitation of the older worker; the recognition of the older volunteer; the discovery of the older learner. We first need briefly to clarify the meaning of health and health effects, in order to discuss the role of purposive activity in these three areas. We also need to understand something of the context of older people's current and projected health status in order to see how activity and productivity could impact, or be seen as significant, in a larger picture.

It has been observed (Minichiello *et al.* 1996: 369) that older people view their health and well-being as inseparable from identities and experiences accumulated throughout life. The value of research into these matters, these authors claim, is that it illuminates meanings of health actions carried out in the context of everyday lives. It can therefore help to formulate policies to facilitate healthier ways of life, and the means by which organized interventions can align more closely with older people's motives, enabling them to choose and achieve beneficial change.

In particular, Minichiello and colleagues' research in the Australian state of Victoria sought to describe the health status of older people, with the aim of establishing a database for health promotion purposes. The emphasis in their data collection (from over 1,000 elders, aged 65 plus, in the community) was on understanding how people formed and changed their patterns of physical activity, social activity, eating patterns and other lifestyle factors known to have health impacts. Adding information on personal and social resources, class and neighbourhood, outcomes were analysed in terms of well-being, independence and service use. Following some previous British research (Blaxter 1990), questioning included items on people's *health ideals*, perceived *health benefits* and *health actions*.

In each of these areas of response, great importance was laid on activity. That is, older people saw physical activity as a prime indicator of *ideal health*; it was also cited as an important *benefit*, along with positive attitude and independence; physical activity was also seen as one of three health *actions* one could take to improve health. Thus, activity played significant parts in self-rated health as both means and outcome. Furthermore, the authors observed that although avoiding disease and preventing dependence were key policy objectives for professionals, they were *not* cited by older people as primary motives for maintaining health. The motivators for people themselves were to achieve and/or maintain well-being and activity.

Turning now to indicators of a non-self assessed kind, Jarvis and Tinker

(1999) have analysed national data from a 15-year period in order to describe trends in morbidity and disability in Britain. They note that although over half the total expenditure on hospital and community health services is spent on those aged 65 and over, it is accepted that greater use denotes greater need, and there is still a high level of support for the redistribution of such resources between people and across generations. Jarvis and Tinker set out to examine the notion that future health costs can be projected on the basis of population change alone, which assumes that the age-related nature of service usage will remain unchanged.

Trends in health status are analysed under two main headings: limiting chronic illness (which is currently declining) and functional disability (which is stable). Data were drawn from the General Household Survey and a number of other periodicals and occasional statistical series, the inclusion and comparison of which were carefully discussed by the authors. Just over 40 per cent of older people (65 plus) report a chronic condition that limits their activities in some way. Within this population, the experience of limiting illness is clearly age-related, moving from about 30 to 60 per cent through age groups 60–64 to 85–89. Gender differentials, which are small at younger ages, also increase with age, with proportionately more older women reporting illness of this kind. Most interestingly, trends over time in these measures show an overall rise in chronic illness until the late 1980s, and then a decline.

In contrast, figures on functional disability, said by the authors to be more objective a measure, have changed little over the review period. Based on degrees of ability to carry out a range of tasks, the overall rate remains at two-thirds of all older people being able to function with no disability, and around one in five having moderate difficulty with one of the named tasks. At all ages within the overall age group, women have slightly higher levels of disability and, as with chronic illness, the experience of disability is clearly age-related for both genders. For severe disability and in the oldest age group only, the male–female gap narrows, i.e. slightly more men report difficulty in this category in this age group.

Why is chronic illness apparently declining, while functional disability is remaining much the same? Jarvis and Tinker conclude that these measures represent different aspects of morbidity and are not necessarily contradictory. Indeed, the complexity of disentangling the many factors in the experience of health and illness is high, and their interpretation to produce trends using cross-sectional data is exceptionally difficult. However, the value of such an exercise is also high, and having discussed some technical factors in data capture and comparison, they go on to venture that improving health can indeed be detected and predicted:

There is a real possibility that smoking cessation, decrease in the consumption of dietary fat, moderate alcohol consumption, seat belt use, regular exercise, which is occurring slowly but on a massive scale, is having an effect on the reduction of old age morbidity.

(Jarvis and Tinker 1999: 619)

Let us look at our 'productive' third ager, to see whether it is the purposive nature of the activity that keeps her or him healthy, bringing with it social and mental engagement; or whether it is increased levels of general health and strong economic factors that are facilitating different types of engagement from those retirement previously offered. It is proposed that alongside the 'busy ethic' of retirement which related to the third age notion of fulfilment through work *and/or* leisure, there is now a 'healthy ethic' related to productive ageing that is becoming the dominant model for later life. The aim is to stay fit, to stay young, to put off retirement until the fourth age when the limiting conditions and disabilities described above finally become the rationale to relinquish the work role.

The rehabilitation of the older worker

Is continuing to work in later life good for people? First in its favour is that it enables the 'worker' to occupy the moral high ground in society, in the immediate community, and in her or his own estimation and identity. There is no major discontinuity with the past, a less challenging change to negotiate, perhaps. However, this 'ethically better' position (Moody 1998) is not without risks, and therefore anxieties. The transition to non-worker has not been done, and may arrive at short notice when the work or the health runs out. The pre-retirement plan needs to expand at both ends to become a flexible life plan, able to respond to several kinds of change. Moody (1998: 329) notes that, as Western societies review the meaning of retirement, they need 'to design social institutions that can open up new possibilities for productive aging. Making better use of the talents of older people would represent a new social policy goal for [American] society.'

Meanwhile, older people are taking the risks as well as reaping the benefits of keeping going in the ways they know best, and in some new ways too. Moody (1998: 326) quotes a US national survey of 3,000 over-55s, in 1991, which found more than 70 per cent of over-55s actively contributing to society: 27 per cent were in paid work; 26 per cent were volunteering; 42 per cent were helping children or grandchildren; 29 per cent were assisting the sick or disabled. The total value of their contributions was estimated as being of equivalent to that of 12 million full-time workers; in care-giving activities alone it was seen as equivalent to 7 million workers. A further 31 per cent were reported as not employed but wishing to be. Moody notes that the greying of the workforce generally requires of employers a changed attitude to the provision of ongoing training and employee development. He sees that greater appreciation of the potential of productive ageing will help to create the new social institutions referred to in the quote above – a picture of second and third careers, community service employment, volunteer opportunities and continuing education and training.

In their discussion of how to achieve a 'productive ageing society', Caro *et al.* (1993) note that some aspects of older people's productivity is better supported because it is expected, such as caring for others, whereas in other less expected areas, such as paid work or some forms of volunteering, they encounter significant barriers. To create wider opportunities, then, the tasks are to reverse the scepticism of employers about older people's capabilities and their own lack of confidence in their ability to be effective workers. Predicting that the labour market will need to turn to 'non-traditional' groups in the light of fewer younger workers, Caro *et al.* recommend that employers not only start removing the barriers to older workers but also help construct ways of accessing work. They have in mind such things as third age career counselling, the viewing of retirement as a transitional not a terminal phase, the redesign of training processes and formats to make them more older-adult friendly, part-time, flexible and unconventional work hours.

They identify four types of barriers to work and volunteering: institutional ageism; cultural lag (slowness in adjusting our expectations to social conditions older people now experience); defective institutions (work and volunteering options are flawed and will be avoided if possible); alternative preferences (there are more attractive things to do than work given the choice). There are obvious implications for those who are keen to see older people staying or becoming productive, to make these options more attractive. Proposing and publicizing health benefits would have a significant part to play in such a strategy. Caro *et al.* writing in 1993, were not recommending that if inducements were not effective then obligations should be increased.

> We would not endorse proposals to expand work obligations or reduced pensions for the elderly, premised on an extended work life. A great deal has to be accomplished in extending work opportunities before there is a sound basis for debating whether work obligations should be increased.

Another angle on the trend of encouraging older worker participation is to emphasize the right to work regardless of age, to resist treating older people as marginal participants in the labour market and campaign for a level playing field of opportunity. Research in this vein has analysed the weaknesses in thinking and in practice that continue to exclude older workers, and the kinds of changes necessary to improve matters (see, for example, Taylor and Walker 1998, for a review of British research, and Montgomery *et al.* 1990, for a discussion of the US values underpinning policy towards older workers).

Finally, on the prospects for the older worker, we return to Phillipson's observation of the link between the emergence of positive health effects of work and periods of discouraged retirement, which, despite its cynical implication, is rather difficult to resist. Phillipson (1993) cites evidence for this thesis, from the 1950s onwards. A recent example of this linkage would be Crimmins *et al.* (1999), who investigated self-reported ability to work, presence of disease and causes of work limitation. They found a significant improvement in the ability to work at age 60 plus, over the ten-year period studied. They conclude that the legislated rise in age of full eligibility for social security benefits should be more than compensated for by the improved ability to work. For further reading on this link, see Abramson *et al.* (1994), who also make a positive association between overall job satisfaction and the health of middle-aged and older workers, especially with regard to occupational factors and psychological strain; and Soumerai and Avorn

(1983), who document the positive effects of part-time employment on life satisfaction and the health of retired people.

The recognition of the older volunteer

In 1991 it was estimated that about a third of people over 65 gave help to someone living outside their own household and, although this declined with age, 8 per cent of men and 6 per cent of women aged 85+ claimed to do so. Tinker (1996) described the main ways and to whom such help is given. These were: *to family*, including children, grandchildren, spouses and to even older parents or other family members (helping roles could be informal or formal, such as being a main carer or support in the community, or having a wardship or power of attorney); *to neighbours*, which varied according to community and neighbourhood type; *through voluntary work roles*, which again varied in degrees of formality and in types of work done; *through civic and political roles*, from standing for public office to exercising one's right to vote.

On the propensity to volunteer, Tinker concludes that social expectations, a perception of being wanted and capable, and economic pressures on family members requiring support are all likely to increase non-paid work. Negative effects on rates of volunteering are the greater need to earn income, a low perceived value of the unpaid contribution or a view of retirement that is incompatible with work of any kind. Tinker does not emphasize the role of health in such activity, because her purpose is to describe the benefits to others of older people's contributions. A paper by Young and Glasgow (1998) does have this emphasis, however, and claims to demonstrate that participation in 'voluntary formal associations' is health enhancing and that this can be supported by evidence from a number of areas.

Having defined voluntary formal association, the authors propose that such involvement appears to improve health over and above other general social benefits, and that the link to voluntary organizations represents a different principle at work compared to the effects of informal contacts. Health measures adopted in various parts of this multifaceted study include lower mortality, perceived health and self-assessed health support. In claiming a particular health benefit of formal voluntary association, the authors reject objections that have been raised to other more general studies of the health-related value of social integration. In particular, their link is claimed to be demonstrated 'net' of any other kinds of informal ties or support. In other words, it really was the active participation in a purposive activity that was beneficial to health. Moreover, a strong association between self-rated health and mortality was found. The policy implications of these two findings alone are profound.

It is a cause for concern, then, to hear of emerging evidence that rates of volunteering among older people are indeed decreasing, probably due to the need to supplement or replace previous earnings (Johnson 1997). For an international perspective on policies and programmes on senior volunteering see Baldock (1999), who, along with others, expresses the hope that initiatives such as the UN Year of Older People will enhance the perception of the value of senior volunteering, while recognizing the economic and political contexts in which programmes must function.

The discovery of the older learner

The range of literature demonstrating the general well-being effects of learning in later life is growing, but is beyond the scope of this chapter. A helpful overview of practice, policy and thinking in this general area is provided by Carlton and Soulsby (1999). Its inclusion as a topic here is to support the notion that participation in employment and volunteering in today's changing society increasingly relies on the ability and opportunity to learn and retrain as often as required. Most writers on productive ageing exclude 'learning for learning's sake', or for leisure and pleasure, from its definition, assigning such activity to the constructive rather than the productive. However, in the risk society, as we have seen, there is less distinction between self-improvement and employability, between vocational and non-vocational. Later life survival skills will require a mixed menu of personal and 'professional' learning, including those of managing change and adapting to new circumstances.

Older learners, like older volunteers and older workers, see health benefits in their engagement. Health reasons, both mental and physical, are cited as primary motivators for participation in learning in later life, expressed particularly in terms of maintaining fitness through stimulation and exercise (Walker 1999). There are also socially generated benefits to well-being from meeting and interacting with others, combating isolation and boredom. Older people are well aware of the value of a positive outlook and self-confidence, as well as the need to keep informed and up to date, all of which are available in a learning situation that recognizes mature experience and seeks to build on existing understanding.

Although a longstanding belief of adult educators, evidence of positive health effects of continuing learning has been more practice-based than theory-tested, more anecdotal than systematically evaluated, because of the difficulty in isolating the numerous factors. Evidence is now emerging from Institute of Employment Studies research, reported early in 2000, that learning can be linked to specific, measurable health outcomes. Exciting as this prospect is, it may be that the success or otherwise of educational programmes is still small in its effect on well-being compared to the individual and day-to-day learning we all do making sense of life experiences and meeting the challenges of change.

We return to the notion that older people view their health as inseparable from identities and experiences built up through life (Minichiello *et al.* 1996). Health promotion will benefit from focusing on the views of older people themselves, as adult educators have had to do. Offering answers to questions that no one is asking and services that people do not connect with their lives is clearly ineffective in promoting health, or any other desirable outcomes. As in education, we need to discover people's (health) goals – their ideals and aspirations – in context. Health benefits need to be recognized and achievable, bearing in mind the difficulties and costs involved. From this, a pattern of health actions may be built up, but these are going to be sensitive to culture, gender, class, neighbourhood etc. As with learning and earning, feeling the benefits and seeing the possibilities are the greatest motivators to carrying on and driving change forward towards greater health.

References

Abramson, J., Gofin, H., Habib, J. and Noam, G. (1994) *Work Satisfaction and Health in the Middle-aged and Elderly*, Jerusalem: JDC-Brookdale Institute of Gerontology and Development.

Baldock, C. V. (1998) Seniors as volunteers: an international perspective on policy, *Ageing and Society*, 19: 581–602.

Blaxter, M. (1990) *Health and Lifestyles*. London: Tavistock Routledge.

Carlton, S. and Soulsby, J. (1999) *Learning to Grow Older and Bolder*. Leicester: National Institute of Adult Continuing Education

Caro, F. G., Bass, S. A. and Chen, Y-P. (1993) *Achieving a Productive Aging Society*. Westport, CT: Greenwood.

Coleman, A. and Chiva, A. (1992) *Coping with Change: Focus on Retirement*. London: Health Education Authority.

Crimmens, E. M., Reynolds, S. L. and Saito, Y. (1999) Trends in health and ability to work among the older working population, *Journal of Gerontology*, 54B(1): S31–40.

Ekerdt, D. J. (1986) The busy ethic: moral continuity between work and retirement, *The Gerontologist*, 26(3): 239–44.

Friedmann, L. J. and Havighurst, R. J. (1954) *The Meaning of Work and Retirement*. Chicago: University of Chicago Press.

Harris, D. (1990) *The Sociology of Aging*, 2nd edn. New York, Harper & Row.

Henley Centre (1998) *Next Generation*. Oxford: Henley Centre.

Jarvis, C. and Tinker, A. (1999) Trends in old age morbidity and disability in Britain, *Ageing and Society*, 19: 603–27.

Johnson, M. (1997) Generational equity and the reformulation of retirement, *Scandinavian Journal of Social Welfare*, 6: 162–7.

Laczko, F. and Phillipson, C. (1991) *Changing Work and Retirement*. Buckingham: Open University Press.

Laslett, P. (1989) *A Fresh Map of Life*. London: Weidenfeld & Nicolson.

Minichiello, V., Chappell, N., Kendig, H. and Walker, A. (1996) *Sociology of Aging: International Perspectives*. Melbourne: International Sociological Association Research Committee on Aging.

Montgomery, R., Borgatta, E., and Koloski, K. (1990) Social policy towards the older worker, in I. Bluestone, R. Montgomery and J. Owen (eds) *The Aging of the American Workforce*. Detroit: Wayne State University Press.

Moody, H. (1998) *Aging, Concepts and Controversies*. Beverly Hills, CA: Pine Forge Press.

Osgood, N. (1982) *Life After Work: Retirement, Leisure, Recreation and the Elderly*. Westport, CT: Greenwood.

Phillipson, C. (1993) The sociology of retirement, in J. Bond, P. Coleman and S. Peace (eds) *Ageing in Society*, 2nd edn. London: Sage.

Soumerai, S. B. and Avorn, J. (1993) Perceived health, life satisfaction and activity in urban elderly – a controlled study of the impact of part-time work, *Journal of Gerontology*, 38(3): 356–62.

Taylor, P. and Walker, A. (1998) Employers and older workers: attitudes and employment practices, *Ageing and Society*, 18: 641–58.

Tinker, A. (1996) *Older People in Modern Society*, 3rd edn. Harlow: Longman.

Walker, J. (1996) *Changing Concepts of Retirement: Educational Implications*. Aldershot: Ashgate.

Walker, J. (1999) 50+ learning, a consultation exercise. Paper presented to the Annual Conference of British Society of Gerontology, Bournemouth, 17–19, September.

Young, F. and Glasgow, N. (1998) Voluntary and social participation and health, *Research on Aging*, 20(3): 339–62.

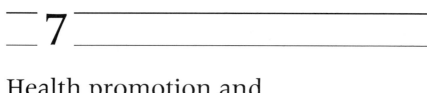

7

Health promotion and sexuality in later life

___ MARY DAVIES _____

Introduction

Relationships with other people are a very important part of life. Pleasure (and pain) can be gained from many kinds of relationships, with partners, family, friends, colleagues and neighbours. These contacts with other human beings can be life enriching and add to one's sense of well-being and belonging.

For many people fulfilling the sexual part of themselves is just as important, and this desire and need does not disappear just because the fiftieth birthday is reached or the decision to retire is made. Sadly, attitudes still abound which suggest that it does, or it should. Yet in later life fulfilling one's sexuality can make life worth living and consequently have a positive effect on health and well-being. This area is still a neglected part of health promotion for older people because of the complex social and psychological factors that operate on individuals and society.

Dealing with these myths and fantasies and replacing them with the facts is an issue for health promotion. In order to do this health professionals need themselves to know the facts about sex and older people, including:

- the effect of ageing on sexual functioning;
- common problems which can arise;
- strategies for dealing with the problems;
- the need for older people to be aware of their own attitudes towards sex and older people.

Changes in sexual response with age

Various research, including work by Pfeiffer *et al.* (1972), has suggested that the following occurs:

1 A decline in sexual activity interest is common with ageing but some people maintain the same level and others increase their levels.
2 Elderly men are more sexually active than elderly women but the primary cause is that men are more likely than women to have a socially sanctioned sexually active partner.

Most of the married women who had ceased to have regular sex indicated that this was because their husbands were no longer capable of sexual activity. Married men who ceased sex generally accepted the responsibility themselves.

There are many factors affecting these research studies. The samples usually consist of a mixture of people who have and always did have varying sex drives. Sex is still a taboo subject and few people are used to talking openly and honestly about it. The attitudes of the researcher and subject will affect the responses. Despite these drawbacks, research results indicate that for those who have been active in youth, growing older does not abolish the need, the capacity or the satisfaction – unless they are affected by illness or deprived of a partner.

The 'now elderly' grew up in a climate of sexual repression, especially for women. It is likely that elderly people of the future, who grew up in a much more positive climate regarding sex, will be less affected by ageing.

Barriers to sexual fulfilment in later life

Prejudice

The greatest barrier to sexual fulfilment is, as already indicated, prejudice. Prejudice presents an almost insurmountable barrier for a great many elderly people even when they have a partner. Comfort (1990) alleges that 75 per cent of the sexual disabilities of older people are sociogenic and their remedy depends on changed attitudes on the part of society and the people themselves. There is some evidence (Gibson 1992) to suggest that after the absence of sexual activity there can be difficulty in beginning again. For people who have been without a partner for some time their doubt about their 'capabilities' may be a barrier to taking a potential sexual relationship further.

Lack of communication and embarrassment

Women who are used to their partner taking the initiative sexually may find that if he stops making sexual overtures (for whatever reason) they may leave it at that. So the sexual lives of older women may well be determined by the inclination and sexual capacity of their partners. Impotence can be caused by various illnesses and disabilities. This will often be so discouraging to the man that he gives up sex, which is 'only what is to be expected at his age'. If his partner is unwilling or unable to talk about this, and unless both of them find ways of resolving the difficulty, then their sex life will cease. So attitudes about what is sexually appropriate for men and women can act as a barrier, as can a lack of communication between couples. Many couples never talk about their sex life even if it has been enjoyable. This is fine while all is well, but if a problem occurs, not being able to talk about it is a barrier to resolving it.

Lack of a partner

There are even greater barriers to emotional and sexual fulfilment for those who do not have a partner. There are about three million women to approximately 800,000 men, i.e. a one in four chance for a women of finding a heterosexual partner. So older women have fewer options than older men for heterosexual companionship, intimacy and sexuality. There are also older men without partners, despite the odds in their favour.

So how can the many older people who are alone find sexual gratification? Mary Stott (1981) suggests a compassionate solution to this problem:

> It seems to me unimaginable and unfeeling to talk about the desirability of sex to people who may wince in pain from the love passage on the television screen or find an old love song brings stinging tears to the eyes. What is much more helpful is to encourage lonely people, older women as well as older men, to accept the idea of masturbation without embarrassment or disgust. I can see no valid objection to it, though I fully sympathise with the many men and women who think it is a poor substitute for sexual intercourse with a loving partner.

Attitudes to masturbation

In the Starr and Weiner (1981) survey the following question was asked: 'Many older people masturbate to relieve sexual tension. What do you think about this?' Eighty-five per cent of women and 70 per cent of men in the survey accepted masturbation. However, of those who accepted it in principle, far fewer admitted to doing it themselves. Many believed masturbation was a positive, healthy and necessary form of sexual release, though some continued to be inhibited by attitudes formed many years ago and were unable to bridge the gap between the idea of masturbation and actually masturbating. Not surprisingly, some people who masturbated had ambivalent feelings about it or felt guilty. These feelings about masturbation were sometimes about self-pleasuring, since for some people it was acceptable within a relationship but not alone. Yet many older people will not have had sexual partners for many years and, as Stott and others have said, 'if it brings relief, comfort and sweet sleep what is the objection to it?' Women may not have acknowledged their own sexual desires. Yet many are now in the position where there is no man to initiate sex, so they need to find alternative means of sexual expression. Attitudes to masturbation and the use of fantasy and sex aids may be another barrier. In the Starr and Weiner survey people were asked: 'How can older people deal with their sexual feelings if they are not married or do not have partners?' Seventeen per cent of men and 37 per cent of women answered by suggesting diversionary activities; 33 per cent of men suggested finding a partner; only 15 per cent of women suggested this, probably realizing the odds were against them; and 22 per cent of women and 20 per cent of men suggested masturbation as a solution. Masturbation may not be the answer to sexual fulfilment for many older people, but for those who do enjoy it the thought that other people may have feelings of disgust or rejection may be a barrier for them.

Loneliness

As well as a sexual need, even more powerful for many people is the need for affectionate touch – a hug, a kiss, a cuddle, not necessarily from someone of the opposite sex. Yet their lives are such that this becomes very difficult to obtain. Many older people behave in an extremely proper way and do not believe that hugs and kisses are acceptable between friends. They may well be kept for grandchildren, but not all older people are grandparents and many do not see their families often. Lots of older people spend hours alone when just up the road is another person also alone, who could become a friend. So much violence is shown on television that many older people are fearful of venturing out alone, especially after dark, and this obviously curtails their opportunities for social contact. The need for physical contact can be especially difficult for older men. What is an affectionate touch and hug from an older woman can from a man illicit responses of 'he's a dirty old man' and suspicion of sexual abuse. Many elderly people do not invite others to their homes even when the home is delightful and they are perfectly capable of making a meal or at least providing a cup of tea or a glass of sherry. If they don't wish to meet friends in the local pub there is often no other venue available where they can sit in warmth and comfort and build up and enjoy a relationship. This will present another barrier to the fulfilment of emotional and sexual needs. A further barrier to the setting up of the stable relationship or marriage has been a fear that the partner will become disabled or infirm and require looking after by the more able person. Older women are often reluctant to take this on again in later life. The same can apply to chores such as ironing shirts and cooking regular meals. Furthermore, marriage may result in the loss of a widow's pension or other means of financial independence, and some older people would not countenance cohabitation for a variety of reasons, ranging from religious belief to anxiety about what the family and neighbours might think. Interestingly, in the Starr and Weiner survey 96 per cent of the men and 86 per cent of the women approved of older people who were not married having sexual relations or living together. However, there is still the problem of finding a partner compounded by the fact that most people meet their partners in the work setting and this is no longer available to most older people.

Homosexual and lesbian relationships

If there are barriers to heterosexual contact in older people there are even greater barriers to homosexual and lesbian relationships. It is relatively recently that homosexual relationships have been made legal and for many people they are still not acceptable, particularly to older people who grew up when homosexuality was a criminal offence. Many older women form close loving relationships with other women yet never transfer their feelings into any form of physical expression. Overcoming these barriers could be a way of providing affectionate touch or someone to share a bed.

Children

An enormous barrier for older people are the attitudes of their children or of other family members, the reason being a fear on their part of the loss of their inheritance. Even when there is no inheritance problem, children can inhibit their parents by strongly disapproving of a potential or actual sexual relationship. This is particularly relevant if one parent is ill or disabled. In the case of the widow or widower, the children may resist them forming new relationships out of some sort of loyalty to their deceased parent even if it is at the expense of the parent still living. This may have more to do with their own feelings of guilt for the dead parent than concern about the living one.

Lack of information

A further barrier for elderly people is to do with their lack of information about giving and receiving sexual pleasure. Many of them had little or no sex education and have not taken the opportunity to read one of the many excellent books currently available. They may mainly see sex and sex roles in a stereotypical way, backed up by romantic stories in the Mills and Boon series. By seeing opportunities for sexual fulfilment in such a narrow way, doors will remain closed on their potential appreciation of sensuality and alternative means of sexual expression.

Professionals

The professionals that older people come into contact with may act as a barrier to their fulfilling their emotional and sexual needs. It is a rare doctor who asks his young patients about sexual difficulties and an even rarer one who asks them if their are no longer young. During training in medical school sexuality is barely mentioned. Sexuality and disability and sexuality in later life are conspicuously absent from the curriculum. Because it is absent from the doctor's curriculum, he or she then assumes that sex isn't in the curriculum for older people, often with sad results.

Sexual problems in later life

The fear of failing is a very powerful barrier. The most frequent cause of impotence is an experience of impotence. Many men withdraw contact rather than face the embarrassment and disappointment, to say nothing of the frustration of another 'failure'. For both men and women there is the fear of rejection and ridicule by their families and the myth of the sexless older life can become a self-fulfilling prophecy.

Just like anyone else at any time of life, older people can have a sexual problem. Its cause may be multifactoral, with age playing only a small part or no part at all. That which is a sexual problem to one person is of no concern to another, but professionals need to 'give permission' to older people to enable them to express their sexual concerns. Many older people would find it difficult to know what language to use to explain the problem to a doctor and, for all the reasons already discussed, would need to be very self-confident or very desperate to raise the subject with an unsympathetic professional. This means that many older people who have problems which could be resolved shy away from seeking help, with consequent loss to themselves and their partners. Although no diseases result directly from ageing itself, many illnesses and disabilities are more common in later life, and alongside this is the fact that many older people are taking some form of medication which may cause sexual problems.

There are some disabilities which occur in later life that do have a direct effect on sexual functioning. In the man it may be difficult or impossible to get an erection or to ejaculate and in the woman vaginal lubrication may not increase as an accompaniment to sexual arousal. These direct effects occur when the spinal cord or the nerves passing from the spinal cord to the sex organs are affected by illness or disability. This can occur after a spinal injury or when the nerves are affected in multiple sclerosis or diabetes mellitus. Another situation in which these effects can occur is when there is nerve damage after surgery, such as after a colostomy, when the nerves passing from the spinal cord to the penis have been affected either by a pre-existing cancer or by the surgery. Fortunately, there are only a few illnesses and disabilities which have these direct effects on sexual functioning.

Information is needed by a couple when one or other has had a stroke or a heart attack. If they are not given the appropriate information, then the resultant fear of the effect of sexual activity will be enough to restrict this part of their lives and perhaps remove it altogether. At the time of discharge from hospital many patients do not feel able to ask questions about the resumption of their sex life and are often just glad to be alive and happy to be going home. Yet if they do not get the information at this point it becomes much more difficult to obtain, so they may be denied it altogether. There is the myth that sexual activity is a very energetic process and it is dangerous for someone who has had a heart attack or a stroke. This is not the case and if the person concerned is sufficiently rehabilitated to be able to climb two flights of stairs then sexual activity should not be dangerous. It may be a good idea for there to be a change in sex roles so that the person that has had the heart attack or the stroke adopts a more passive role in the sexual activity, the active role being taken by the partner. It is also a good idea to enjoy sexual relationships in a relaxed atmosphere and environment and not to have a hot bath, too much alcohol or a heavy meal beforehand.

Lack of or limited body control

This can occur after a stroke when the individual is left with partial paralysis. New positions for sexual intercourse need to be tried in order to find one which is comfortable and possible for both individuals. Arthritis affects many older people. It often occurs in women in the hip joints and when this does occur it may be painful for the woman to lie with her legs spread apart. So sexual intercourse in this position may be difficult or in some cases impossible. Usually, sexual intercourse is possible in some alternative positions, but many couples need information and reassurance about this, since they may not feel it is appropriate for them.

Incontinence

A particular loss of control which is very much feared in later life is that of incontinence of both the bladder and bowel. This is a lack of bladder or bowel control. It can cause problems in several ways. First, there can be practical problems; second, there can be emotional and psychological ones. Incontinence can be viewed by the individual or partner with extreme distaste and in some situations people are too ashamed even to admit to the problem, so seeking help is just not within their remit.

In the practical sense, leakage of urine during sexual intercourse can be inconvenient to say the least, and individuals may well find comfort in being given information about this (i.e. don't drink too many cups of tea or pints of beer before sexual intercourse). Some people believe that urine leakage will harm their partner or themselves. In most cases fresh urine is sterile, so it should not harm either partner. Where there is an infection, however, treatment should be sought. When a catheter is worn some people are frightened that during sexual intercourse it may be dislodged, and many are not even aware that sexual intercourse can be experienced while the catheter is in place. This can occur by taping it in position and experimenting to find a position that is comfortable for both partners. If the catheter is worn by the man it can be bent back over the shaft of the penis and taped in place when the man has an erection or held in place by a sheath. Positions for sexual intercourse can be found so that neither partner is lying on the tubing of the catheter.

Another problem of incontinence is that it can lead to feelings of negative body image and anxieties about personal attractiveness. Every attempt needs to be made to inspire confidence to ensure that individuals have the best possible aids and equipment to cope with their incontinence. Another aspect of dealing with the problem is to plan for sexual activity a little ahead so that the bladder is emptied in the usual way before sexual activity, and diuretic drinks such as tea and coffee or alcohol are restricted for a few hours prior to love-making.

Bowel incontinence is extremely distressing to older people and can mean the end of an active sex life. Often when people have a stoma and a bag to cope with sex can seem to present just another set of problems. Yet if they can be overcome the benefits are great: a validation of the person as a sexual individual, the comfort and delight of skin to skin contact and the assurance that one is still part of the wider sexual world. Reassurance and information are required. Sex will not harm the stoma, and bags can be obtained which don't leak and fit well. The bag needs to be emptied before sex, with great attention being paid to personal hygiene and ensuring that there is no smell. The bag and stoma could be covered during love-making if that enhances the feeling of attractiveness of the individual. Many people feel they look more sexy in pretty underwear or boxer shorts. Various positions for sex need to be tried to find the most comfortable, and some attention to diet may be a good idea so that food which is more problematic is avoided for some hours before sex.

The effect of drugs

Many older people frequently visit their doctor and are taking prescribed drugs and in some cases several drugs. Some of these drugs cause sexual difficulty. The extent of the problem is difficult to calculate but, according to Davies and D'Mello (1985), it is likely to be substantial.

Drugs can clearly affect libido. This may be put down to getting older by both the older person and his or her doctor. The problems may be particularly significant, since it has been well established that older people have a response to many drugs that is missing in younger adult patients. This is likely to be because of a lower rate of excretion and metabolism of the drug.

Other drugs cause arousal problems – that is, impotence in men – including beta-blockers, which many older men take to reduce their high blood pressure. Many men who are now impotent are unaware that their impotence was probably first caused by beta-blocking pills. Other drugs cause problems with orgasm, including several anti-depressants: imiparamine and protriptyline can cause delayed or decreased ejaculation.

The sexual side-effects of many drugs have not been clearly established, since they are not considered by doctors and the patient does not necessarily make the connection between the onset of the problem and the prescribing of the drug. Many of these drugs may be essential to the well-being of the older patient, but at what price? There may be alternative drugs which have less drastic side-effects. If there are no alternative drugs then at least the patient should be told the potential side-effects so that he or she doesn't see it as a personal failure or emotional or psychological problem. It can also be very helpful for partners concerned to have this information so that they do not see themselves as unattractive and failing in their duty as sexual partners.

Solutions to these problems

In some instances, because of the illness or disability changed sexual function cannot be restored. For example, a man who has multiple sclerosis may not be able to get an erection due to the effect of the disease on the nerves passing to the penis, and no amount of sexual therapy will alter this. However, this does not mean that the individual is not able to have a sex life. There is a great deal more to enjoying sex for many people than simply having sexual intercourse and one of the most oppressive myths in our society, which is still widely held, is that there is only one way to have a sexual relationship. Many men who are unable to get an erection, either temporarily or permanently, feel devastated and believe that they have nothing to offer in a sexual relationship. The same may be true for women who, for one reason or another, are not able to have penetrative sex with their partner. They fear their partner will leave them because of the lack of sexual fulfilment, and will be looking for a 'proper' sexual partner elsewhere.

To feel unable to provide sexual satisfaction for one's partner because of such problems is very disabling and reduces the quality of life for older people. However, many women find it a good deal easier to experience an orgasm by love-making which does not involve sexual intercourse, such as masturbation and oral sex. Many men enjoy masturbation not just during their adolescence but throughout the whole of their lives. So even if sexual intercourse is not possible it is still possible to have and to give a great deal of sexual pleasure.

It is helpful to remember the importance of skin to skin contact and the reassurance and pleasure that can be given and obtained by a hug and a kiss.

Sex aids

Some men find aids to obtaining and maintaining an erection extremely useful and satisfying. The Blako ring or energizing ring has copper and zinc electrodes set into either end. The ring is placed around the base of the penis and must be the correct size, since it needs to fit accurately in order to be effective. It encourages the erection by its slight constrictive effect on the penile veins, although it may also have a powerful psychological effect. It is not always effective, in which case the artificial penis may be a useful aid. This consists of an erect latex penis which is hollow and placed over the man's own non-erect penis and held in place by hand or with various straps. When using this aid to sexual intercourse, it is more comfortable if lubrication is provided by smearing the artificial penis with K-Y jelly. Couples have found the use of this particular sex aid a great enhancement to their love-making. It can also be used by a woman on her own or with another woman.

Another useful sex aid is the vibrator, which contains a battery and when turned on vibrates either gently or more powerfully and so acts as a powerful stimulus. It can be used by a woman alone to enhance masturbation or it can be used by a couple as part of their love-making. It is particularly useful where one of the couple has poor hand movements and cannot stroke the other person. It can be used as a great source of pleasure for stroking the back or other parts of the body. Because it is made of rigid plastic it is not designed for penetration.

The artificial vagina is lined with latex and contains a vibrator. It can be used in several situations: for instance, for a man without a partner or for a couple where the woman is unable to have sexual intercourse, perhaps due to surgery. In this situation the artificial vagina can be held between her thighs and sexual intercourse can take place in this way. Again K-Y jelly is useful as lubrication. In order for sex aids to be a useful way to get around some of the sexual problems both partners need to feel comfortable about their use, in which case they can provide a great deal of pleasure, satisfaction and fun.

It is important to remove goals from love-making, so that problems can be overcome. Orbach (1996) indicates that a more helpful view would be to regard sexual behaviour as a means towards intimacy rather than an end in itself. In conclusion, sex is for real people, whether they are young or old. Everyone has the capability to make love, no matter how old they are or how disabled. Love-making is a means of expressing feelings in ways which are appropriate to the physical capabilities of the individuals concerned. As Moody (1998: 167) suggests, 'Sexual activity in later life is most clearly accounted for by the continuity theory of ageing – the best prediction of sexual behaviour in later life is earlier sexual behaviour.'

Older people in residential accommodation

About 5 per cent of older people live in residential accommodation, the majority of them women. This is a substantial number of people. It is important to consider the implications of residential care, since it can seriously affect the fulfilment of emotional and sexual needs.

For most people, to be able to enjoy sexuality requires access to privacy. This is likely to be particularly so for older people who grew up when sex was a taboo subject, especially for women. Many older people are only too well aware of the attitudes of people in general towards sexuality in later life, and they do not want to be the butt of humour or ridicule. Even when residents do have their own rooms, privacy is not guaranteed. There may not be a lock on the door and staff may walk in without knocking. In some places walls are paper thin and any sound can be heard in the adjoining room, so that it is not even possible to cry in private.

Older people sometimes move into residential accommodation after a stay in hospital. They might have become used to accepting a lack of privacy and continue not even to expect privacy, let alone insist on it as a right. The ethos in some residential establishments doesn't seem to be one in which the notion of human rights can flourish!

Privacy is also curtailed on another level, since it is likely that staff and other residents know who goes into whose room, whether or not they lock the door, how long they stay there and so on. Staff may well feel obliged to report such events to relatives, and then yet another facet of privacy is lost. For many elderly people their sexuality is a very private part of themselves and to have other people aware of how this is fulfilled would be deeply offensive – so they often just put this part of their lives aside.

Sadly, in some homes residents have been prevented from having a fulfilling relationship by the lack of appropriate accommodation, but particularly by the attitudes of staff and other residents and even feared attitudes in the surrounding community.

Since most of the people in residential care are older women it is unlikely that many of them will be able to have a male sexual partner. This does not mean that the sexual needs and feelings of these women just evaporate. Far from it. Some women are able to get a great deal of pleasure from interacting with men who may be much younger than they are and who come into their lives in one way or another. Such relationships or meetings may pass unnoticed by the man concerned but be a great source of delight to the older women. So a resident may get a great deal of pleasure from a young male member of staff or the male doctor or chiropodist. Wherever possible it is important that people of the opposite sex visit the home and maintain social contact.

Coping strategies for staff

Particularly powerful feelings can be evoked in both staff and other residents if anti-social or inappropriate sexual behaviour takes place, such as public masturbation or touching up other residents. Many people respond to overt masturbation by feeling very angry and hostile to the person concerned. They may well not know that the behaviour may be due to an illness such as dementia or a stroke. When it occurs there can be a great deal of embarrassment around and people cope with it by behaving in a very strict and proper way themselves. It may even have the effect of making them disapprove of their own sexual feelings.

Staff can have different professional approaches. Some staff, who often have years of experience, want to run the residential setting on well established and controlled lines. Others want to bring in changes and want the home to reflect the changes in attitudes in society in general. Staff need to work together and can utilize the very different ideas about the way things should be done. These may be influenced by their religion, their culture, their age, their personal experiences and probably a lot of other things besides. Often residential establishments have no agreed policy about responding to the sexual needs of their residents. They may never have discussed them other than in a joke or as a complaint, and may have unresolved feelings and anxieties about the subject of sexuality, particularly that of sexuality in later life. This is compounded by the lack of training which occurs in residential establishments.

Issues for health professionals

The attitudes of conservative doctors and others towards sexuality and older people are vividly outlined by H. B. Gibson (1992). Sexuality in later life is seen very negatively by many, is administratively inconvenient, is a source of embarrassment and creates anxiety about lack of knowledge. Sherman (1999) found that staff identified a range of emotions when dealing with dependent older people, including empathy, sadness, personal vulnerability and a strong desire to suppress emotions such as personal discomfort with sexual matters. Biggs (1993) explores the issues of older people and health and welfare professionals. He asks the question: 'can the projects of older age find a legitimate voice within the common sense worlds inhabited by professional helpers?' (p. 102). As he goes on to point out, 'If practitioners are trained and work in situations where exposure to peers and younger people is the norm, then the concerns of older people may be perceived as deviant.' A further difficulty is that professionals usually work with disadvantaged older people, so do not see the whole picture.

Adelman *et al.* (1991) suggest that health workers need to be aware of two agendas: that of their own professional role, and that arising from the position of the older person. Strong boundaries are required to define misunderstandings which could arise from the intimacy that can be generated by discussing personal health issues.

Professionals need to remember that the faces of older people are 'masks'

(Featherstone and Hepworth 1989) and should not be taken as a signal to 'disattend' the individual. The real person is a sexual person who may be just as romantic and passionate as at any other time in his or her life. Sadly, ageist stereotyping has been found to achieve dominance over sex, occupation and race (Bassili and Riel 1981). According to H. B. Gibson (1992), the responsibility of professional care givers can be summarized under four headings: to organize practical help, to educate, to advise and to give moral support around sexuality in later life.

Health promotion professionals will be able to offer the necessary support if:

1 The attitude is one of acceptance of the sexual needs and wishes of older people. Disapproval can be subtle and surprise even the health professional themselves.
2 They have adequate knowledge of the facts about sexual function and ageing.
3 They understand the barriers to fulfilling sexual needs in later life and how they can be overcome.
4 They understand their own attitudes to aspects of sexuality such as masturbation, homosexual and lesbian relationships and the use of sex aids.
5 They put the subject of sexuality on the agenda and do not leave it to the older person.
6 Where appropriate, a code of practice is established.

Conclusion

According to Biggs (1993), the task for successful existence is the ability to hold an identity together without it being eclipsed by the surrounding chaos. This is very relevant in terms of sexual identity in later life. Starr and Weiner (1992) point out that sex and power are intertwined, so that sexuality will be influenced by the overall status of the older person. However, great changes are taking place and present and future generations of older people are doers and shakers who will find ways of personal and sexual fulfilment, and perhaps solutions and alternatives which will enrich and transform health in later life.

References

Adelman, R. D., Greese, M. G. and Charon, R. (1991) Issues in physician–elderly interaction, *Ageing and Society*, 11: 127–47.
Bassili, J. N. and Riel, J. E. (1981) The dominance of the old age stereotype, *Journal of Gerontology*, 36(6): 682–8.
Biggs, S. (1993) *Understanding Ageing: Images, Attitudes and Professional Practice*. Buckingham: Open University Press.
Comfort, A. (1990) *A Good Age*. London: Pan Books.
Davies, M. A. and D'Mello, A. (1985) *Drugs and Sexual Function: A Pharmacological Approach*. Harpenden: Ridge Publications.
Featherstone, M. and Hepworth, M. (1989) Aging and old age, in B. Bytheway, T. Keil, P. Allat and A. Bryman (eds) *Becoming and Being Old*. London: Sage.

Gibson H. B. (1992) *The Emotional and Sexual Lives of Older People: A Manual for Professionals*. London: Chapman & Hall.

Gibson, T. (1992) *Love, Sex and Power in Later Life: A Libertarian Perspective*. London: Freedom Press.

Kulik, L. and Bareli, H. Z. (1997) Continuity and discontinuity in attitudes towards marital power relations: pre-retired vs. retired husbands, *Ageing and Society*, 17(5): 571–95.

Moody, H. R. (1998) *Ageing Concepts and Controversies*. Beverley Hills, CA: Pine Forge.

Orbach, A. (1996) *Not Too Late: Psychotherapy and Ageing*. London: Jessica Kingsley.

Pfeiffer, E., Verwoedt, A. and Davis, G. C. (1972) Sexual behaviour in middle life, *American Journal of Psychiatry*, 128: 1262–7.

Starr, B. D. and Wiener, M. B. (1981) *The Starr Weiner Report on Sex and Sexuality in the Mature Years*. New York: McGraw Hill.

Sherman, B. (1999) *Sex Intimacy and Aged Care*. London: Jessica Kingsley.

Stott, M. (1981) *Ageing for Beginners*. Oxford: Basil Blackwell.

8

Developing an innovative fall prevention strategy in a primary care setting

— ALISON ALLEN —

This chapter reports a broad-based multi-agency fall prevention strategy within a general practice setting. The initial baseline data will be used to reduce accidents and injuries for older people within a variety of community settings. Results provide important information about older people's views on health promotion activities related to accident prevention and contribute towards the introduction and development of primary care group strategies.

The prevention of accidents has been identified as one of the four key priority areas in the government's public health strategy, *Saving Lives: Our Healthier Nation* (Secretary of State for Health 1999). The key target is to reduce the death rate from accidents by at least one-fifth and to reduce the rate of serious injury from accidents by at least one-tenth by 2010. Accidents, and in particular falls, represent a major cause of death and morbidity among older adults. The effects of major accidents on daily living are described within the Health Education Authority publication *Older People and Accidents* (1999) as contributing significantly to life changes for older people, leading to loss of independence and confidence, with the reduced possibilities for further emotional and physical well-being contributing to low self-esteem and poor mental health. The health and social care consequences represent a serious public health problem, which has been highlighted by Tinetti *et al.* (1988, 1994), Campbell *et al.* (1989, 1997), O'Loughlin *et al.* (1993) and Tinetti (1994).

The Health Education Authority, in *Older People in the Population* (1998), reported that, in 1996, 31 per cent of the population were aged 50 and over, and almost 16 per cent aged 65 and over. By 2026, 41 per cent of the population will be aged over 50, and over 21 per cent of the population will be over pensionable age. The health problems faced by older people have serious consequences for long-term quality of life, which reflect the need for greater health and social care provision.

One of the most serious consequences of falls is hip fracture. The incidence is rising more than would be expected, and is estimated by Dowswell *et al.* (1999) to occur in between 4 and 6 per cent of cases following a fall. The potential health and social care consequences for both the ageing population and the providers of health and social care highlight the need for urgency in the identification of key issues which will result in the development of appropriate strategies for fall prevention.

Cryer (1998) reported falls in people aged over 65 as the principal cause of death (46 per cent of injury deaths) and admission to hospital (59 per cent of all admissions for injury) in the accident category. Cryer *et al.* (1996), discussing the significance of injury in relation to other health problems, stated that 60 per cent of bed days in one region of England, which formed their study population, were taken up as a consequence of fall-related hospital admissions; fractures as a whole (all ages) accounted for 59 per cent of bed days.

In the primary, secondary and tertiary health promotion of accident and injury prevention in older people, it is necessary to ask the question: who is at risk of falling? Dowswell *et al.* (1999), discussing epidemiological studies, showed the characteristics of older people who fall, and the circumstances in which falls occur. They reported that all authors agree that the causes of falls are multifactoral, with two separate types of factors which contribute to falls: first, the characteristics of the individual 'faller'; second, the factors associated with the environment in which the fall occurs.

Sowden *et al.* (1996) reported how very few fall interventions have been rigorously evaluated. Their systematic review of current literature regarding epidemiological studies identified over 400 variables described as potential risk factors for falls. The reviewers identified the interventions that appear to be most effective as those which improve muscle strength and balance, or address the multifactoral causes of falls using a multiple intervention strategy aimed at a number of risk factors.

Fall reduction and exercise programmes

Piotrowski Brown (1999) has suggested that current evidence supports intervention programmes matched to the elderly individual's risk profile, including exercise for strength, balance and gait problems, which can result in significant fall reduction. Adherence to an exercise programme is important, and there are many reasons why older people do not complete the regime. Enjoyable, convenient exercise which offers social support and interaction with a health professional is significant and important in maintaining adherence.

A barrier to older people agreeing to enter exercise programmes is anxiety about dizziness, which contributes to their fear of falling, or actual falling, during exercise sessions. Chair-based exercise (McMurdo and Rennie 1993) enhances the likelihood of older people agreeing to try it out. In fact, potential participants require persuasion that the exercise programme is safe, as well as information relating to its effectiveness for older people.

Other factors which contribute to effectiveness in the design and implementation of exercise programmes include appropriateness, acceptability and adherence. Skelton and McLaughlin (1996) studied the feasibility and acceptability of an exercise class run by health care professionals to examine whether an eight-week period of moderate intensity exercise could improve the strength, flexibility, balance and selected functional abilities of community-living women aged 74 years and over. They confirmed the importance of training for strength using movements which closely mirror everyday activities, rather than training to increase the strength and power of individual muscles. Skelton and Dinan (1999) reviewed the feasibility of exercise for falls management, and highlighted the urgency for further research evidence, models of good practice and guidelines on prevention and treatment initiatives. Such developments inform how we may also extend exercise programmes to home settings. Campbell *et al.* (1997) carried out a randomized controlled trial in a general practice programme of home-based exercise to prevent falls in elderly women aged over 80 years. Results showed that the exercise programme was effective in improving physical function and in reducing falls and injuries.

Getting up after a fall

A well documented hazard associated with falling is the length of time people spend waiting for help to get up. Simpson and Salkin (1993) identified the consequences of fallers lying on the floor for a long period as hypothermia, dehydration, bronchopneumonia and the development of pressure sores. Simpson and Mandelstam (1995) emphasized the importance of restoring confidence in balance ability, and advocated teaching people how to cope with a fall and avoid the 'long lie' associated with such traumas. Many older people had unrealistic ideas regarding their own coping mechanisms, and the researchers stated how success may be increased by using an alternative teaching approach based on errorless learning principles and described as 'backward chaining'. Reece and Simpson (1996) reported that older people at risk of falling become anxious when asked to learn the way to get up from the floor. The conventional method requires people to be helped down to the floor. With the alternative method, participants are not asked if they agree to being taught how to get up from the floor, but if they are willing to learn how to get down to it. The two key principles are that the person should always succeed with each component and that only when individuals could complete each step with ease could they proceed to the next step in the sequence.

More recently, Reece and Simpson (1996) conducted a study which was designed to compare two different methods of teaching people how to get up after a fall. The conclusions from that study influenced the development by Simpson, in consultation with members of AGILE (Association of Chartered Physiotherapists Working with Older People), ACPC (Association of Chartered Physiotherapists in the Community) and OTEP (Occupational Therapists Working with Older People), of guidelines for managing falls among older people (Simpson *et al.* 1998). The guidelines for the collaborative rehabilitative management of elderly people who have fallen have been audited nationally. The four aims of the guidelines are addressed in each component of the fall intervention strategy described within this chapter. The aims are:

1 To improve elderly people's ability to withstand threats to their balance.
2 To improve the safety of their surroundings.
3 To prevent them suffering the consequences of a long lie on the floor, e.g. pressure sores, hypothermia and bronchopneumonia.
4 To optimize their confidence and, wherever relevant, their carers' confidence in their ability to move about as safely and as independently as possible in order to do the things they want to do.

More recent national initiatives include the National Guidelines for the Prevention of Falls in Elderly People, developed on behalf of the Department of Health. The guidelines produced by Feder *et al.* (1998) provided a current literature review, including recommendations which can be implemented in different settings.

The innovative fall prevention strategy

In this section I outline the study itself. Its purpose is to implement and evaluate a multi-agency fall prevention intervention in a general practice setting. The study targets members of the older population who have reported a fall. For the purposes of the study, a fall is defined as 'an event which results in a person coming to rest inadvertently on the ground or lower level and involves a change of position and lack of intention to do so.' It excludes sustaining a violent blow, loss of consciousness, sudden onset of paralysis (e.g. stroke) or an epileptic seizure (Gibson *et al.* 1987; O'Loughlin *et al.* 1993).

The study has two main aims. The first is to examine the effectiveness of a multifactoral intervention in relation to fall prevention which considers both intrinsic and extrinsic risk factors associated with falling. The second is to demonstrate how such an intervention can be incorporated into the practice of health professionals.

The study authors hypothesized that group participants would demonstrate greater physiological and psychological changes than those who did not participate; and that they would experience a lower re-fall rate than those who did not participate. The length of the trial was influenced by two main factors: first, the decision to work with one general practice; second, the actual practice population, which automatically determined the potential number of participants recruited.

Subjects were included in the study if they met the following criteria: aged 65 or over; lived independently in the community; registered with one particular general practice; experienced a fall which fulfilled the accepted study definition of a fall; reported the fall to the primary health care team, or attended an accident and emergency unit; were able to communicate and participate appropriately within each component of the study. Following referral and potential inclusion in the study all patients were contacted and offered a comprehensive post-fall assessment.

Assessment

The following data were collected during initial home-based post-fall assessment:

- *Personal details*, including others living in the same household, carers' details, usual means of transport, financial situation.
- *Home environment*, including steps, stairs, ability to manage them and other environmental concerns such as flooring, as well as security.
- *Medical information*, including existing health problems, lying and standing blood pressure, and urinalysis.
- *Medication review*: prescribed and self-administered medication, including compliance issues collected during all four assessments. In addition, changes in prescribed medication following review at the initial assessment.
- *Physical health*, including activity level, physical functioning and mobility before the fall, and usual walking ability.
- *Personal care ability*, including ability to use the toilet, bath or shower, care for feet and manage dressing.
- *Senses*: hearing, vision and taste.
- *Alcohol* consumption and *smoking* habits.
- *Social functioning* before the accident.
- *Use of services* in the past three months.
- Perceived needs for aids and equipment, e.g. bath and walking aids.
- *Falls history*, including date of last fall, number of falls in previous 12 months, details of last three falls before the referral fall, e.g. exact location and activity at the time and subsequent follow-up action.
- *Occurrences during pre-fall phase*: perceived health in the 14 days before the fall, illness or symptoms of infection at time of fall, alcohol and medication, including PRN medication, such as analgesics to be used as required, in the previous 24 hours.
- *Circumstances of the fall*: type and direction of fall and perceived cause.
- *Summoning help after referral fall*: method of summoning help and time spent on the floor.
- *Outcome and service use*, including details of injuries and fractures.
- *Fear of falling*: Falls Efficacy Scale (modified) (Tinetti *et al.* 1990).
- *Postural stability testing*: see text.
- *Mood assessment*: Hospital Anxiety and Depression Scale (Zigmond and Snaith 1983).

Modification of risk factors associated with falls

One of the aims of the study is the modification of those risk factors known to be associated with falls. Following assessment and identification of risk, referrals are made to appropriate agencies. The potential for referral includes the primary health care team, other health care professionals (such as community physiotherapists, occupational therapists, chiropodists, hearing therapists, specialist nurses and other health service personnel) and statutory and non-statutory agencies (such as social services, local authorities and voluntary agencies).

Medication review

Medication has been identified by Cummings *et al.* (1991), Wagner *et al.* (1994), Close *et al.* (1999) and Cottee (1999) as representing a major risk factor for falls. During each assessment every participant is asked for details of all prescribed and self-medicated drugs. The number, type, dosage and recommended instructions are discussed and actual details of usage and general compliance issues considered. A pharmacist makes recommendations to the appropriate general practitioner. Upon completion of the study it will be possible to report upon the prescribing practices, compliance issues and risk factors for falls, and to describe how this way of working has influenced primary health care team members. This applies especially to concerns in medication-related issues, and to ways in which community pharmacists can work with primary care group professionals to influence appropriate prescribing when considering fall risk.

The three physiological measurements carried out at each assessment were cited by Skelton and McLaughlin (1996). They were a timed get up and go test (Podsiadlo and Richardson 1991), a functional reach test (Duncan *et al.* 1990) and a balance test (Iverson *et al.* 1990).

Psychological assessment

The Hospital Anxiety and Depression Questionnaire (Zigmond and Snaith 1983; Snaith and Zigmond 1994) is a self-administered questionnaire which detects and distinguishes between anxiety and depression. It is applied nine times during the study period, during the initial post-fall assessment (baseline questionnaire) and during further assessments carried out in the home at six, 12 and 18 months. Postal versions are sent to subjects in the intervening and further periods at three, nine, 15, 21 and 24 months.

Re-fall rate

Re-fall rates for community-dwelling study participants have been reported by Campbell *et al.* (1989), Gaeblar (1993), Berg *et al.* (1997) and Close (1999). Within this study, participants are asked to complete and return a falls calendar, which is sent to them each month. Any reported falls result in an independent nurse telephoning them in order to establish that they had experienced a fall which met with the study definition of a fall; and to identify the circumstances, injuries and subsequent outcome regarding the fall. Any participants who do not return their calendar are telephoned and reminded by the same independent interviewer. All participants will be followed up for at least two years.

Randomization

Following assessment and confirmation of inclusion, participants are then age and sex matched and randomly assigned into an exercise and education group or a control group (no exercise or education) after one year. Ethical committee approval was obtained prior to commencement of the study. A second phase of the study includes inviting the original control group into the 'case' (exercise and education) group.

Exercise and discussion groups

Subjects who are selected to enter the exercise programme are invited to attend twice weekly for six months, or 46 sessions, in order to take part in a chair-based progressive strength resistance training programme. The main advantage of the chair-based exercise programme used is that it can be undertaken by anyone despite his or her individual degree of ability or disability.

The exercise programme takes approximately 40 minutes and includes:

- a general warm-up using rhythmic movements;
- gentle mobilizing movements designed to increase range of movement in joints, including trunk rotation and flexion;
- pulse-raising activities;
- stretching exercises involving major muscle groups;
- progressive resistance exercises using Therabands to improve muscle strength.

Functional training

The strong relationship between fear of falling and the restriction of daily living has been identified by Tinetti *et al.* (1988, 1990, 1993, 1994a), Arfken *et al.* (1994), Tinetti (1994), Vellas *et al.* (1997) and Piotrowski Brown (1999). The functional training component of the programme aims to improve weight-bearing functional activity, and includes participants practising rising from a chair, and getting down to and up from the floor following the backward chaining method (Reece and Simpson 1996). Group members regularly observe each other walking and moving around and, through discussion, consider ways in which they could incorporate changes in movement which would maximize their safety as well as contribute to their feelings of confidence. Goal setting on an individual basis, as reported by Allen and Simpson (1999), formed an important motivation for group members. Achieving small goals outside of the group time and reporting progress to group members have been very effective in raising self-esteem and reducing the fear of falling identified by many researchers.

Group discussion

Following the exercise component of the groupwork, group participants are included in group discussion. The focus of the discussion is based upon anything which relates to the risk, event or consequences of falls. Addressing participants' expressed fear of falling is a major recurring theme, and discussion focuses upon instilling or restoring confidence in their own ability to acknowledge their fear and subsequently consider how to tackle it.

Health-related issues are discussed in the whole group or in smaller groups;

they include chiropody, continence, medication, pain, keeping warm, exercise and keeping mobile, sensory impairment, sleep patterns and many others. Other issues concern bereavement and loss, ageing and ageism, contact with others, such as family, friends, neighbours and health professionals, and loneliness.

With regard to attitudes to ageing, illness and falling among the study group, there seemed to be a huge acceptance of 'fate' when subjects discussed the limited degree of control they felt they had over their lives. Tones and Tilford (1994), explaining how central to the state of self-empowerment is a set of psychological attributes that includes beliefs about control, describe the notion of perceived locus of control. Participants felt that one of the groups of people most likely to reinforce their commonly held belief, which reflects an external locus of control, was health and other professionals. Cooper *et al.* (1999) reported fatalism when researching health-related behaviour and attitudes of older people. An apparent increase of fatalism with age has been observed in quantitative studies, and Cooper *et al.* note how individuals' feeling of a lack of control over external forces explains the apparent reluctance of some individuals to modify their health behaviour. However, their secondary analysis of national data sets, which looked at social factors that influence health beliefs and health-promoting behaviour, concluded that, within older age groups, the relationship between age and fatalism was relatively modest and the most important factor was the educational level of the individual. An unknown factor when one considers the barriers and constraints to behaviour change by older people in relation to accident reduction is the effect of specific interventions and, in particular, whether empowering individuals by contributing to their understanding of health risks, while informing them of their potential role in modifying those risk factors, goes some way towards altering their perceived control.

Dodge and Knutesen (cited in Webb 1994) described special teaching strategies for use with older people attending groups. Hearing impairment, when, for instance, people lose the ability to hear high frequencies, represents the greatest challenge, followed by visual impairment and degrees of functional and cognitive ability. Specific diseases, such as arthritis, Parkinson's and varying types and degrees of heart disease, are important considerations with individuals.

One of the important factors used in the intervention that contributes to motivating participants is relating every aspect of the programme to everyday activities, as recommended by Skelton and McLaughlin (1996). This involves explaining to individuals how the activity will help them to go up and down stairs, transfer, reach up, turn around, grip and be more stable, as well as stronger. Explanations are given of why each part of the body or muscle is being exercised and its importance to participants, who are encouraged to feel and understand the difference when muscles are contracted during exercise.

During the groupwork sessions, participants are asked to report how they feel the programme is affecting them in their own environment. The twice-weekly discussion with participants includes current research findings concerning fall risk, as recommended by Downton (1993), with clear explanations given of the reasons why, for instance, older people have a less efficient fall-break response (Maki and McIlroy 1999), accompanied with practical advice about the benefits of improving, for instance, ankle joint mobility (Vandervoort 1999). Explanations increase group interest and improve adherence to the programme.

When participants have completed their 46 sessions over a six-month period, they are invited to attend a monthly reunion where they gradually assume responsibility for the management of the group.

Transferring the study results into local practice

Information gathered in the study regarding fall risk assessment, medication review and subsequent referral to appropriate services will be used in particular to take a targeted approach within a multidisciplinary setting. The initial baseline data were available from mid-2000 and will be used to influence accident and injury reduction for older people within a variety of community settings. Results will provide important information about older people's views regarding health promotion activities related to accident prevention and contribute towards the introduction and development of primary care group strategies in conjunction with the government health strategy, *Saving Lives: Our Healthier Nation*. The strategy highlights the potential for more of a public health approach to accident and injury prevention with older people. The methodology for this study took into account the multifactoral nature of fall risk for older people and therefore subsequent planned interventions will be influenced by multi-agency and multidisciplinary working, which requires recognition and support from a public health agenda approach in order to succeed.

If the results of the exercise programme are positive, and improvements to the postural stability of participants are shown, the case for exercise within fall reduction programmes can be justified and supported by other research findings. The relevance to clinical practice within nursing and health care in a primary care setting can then be demonstrated. As an essential component of primary secondary and tertiary prevention within health and social care planning, consequently, community-based exercise programmes, including home-based initiatives, might be developed within primary care groups.

Evidence surrounding those people who have single falls, in comparison to those who go on to become recurrent fallers, will enable health professionals within primary care groups to assess the extent of the consequences more accurately and to plan a targeted approach to preventive methods.

Challenges

Opportunities for the primary and secondary care sector to work together to implement new recommendations have increased following recent changes. The task of health authorities is to devise health improvement programmes in which to meet the key areas outlined by the latest government strategy, *Saving Lives: Our Healthier Nation*. This has led many people who are eager to use current research to face the inevitable hurdle of transferring research findings into practice. Thompson (1998) highlighted the problems of implementing valid research results into clinical practice and examined recent reviews, which conclude that passive dissemination of information alone is insufficient to improve practice. Further barriers are the administrative or financial policies which exist within organizations and settings and can act as disincentives to improving the practice of individuals. This is of particular relevance to health promotion among older people within a clinical setting, as many programmes within health promotion frameworks, which are supported by national and health authority bodies, have in the past concentrated upon delivering programmes to younger people.

The communication and collaboration challenges, resulting from the main changes within the NHS and social care sector over the past 20 years, have caused difficulties in providing effective services for older people (Iliffe *et al.* 1998). These changes include the introduction of internal markets, screening programmes, community care and a primary care led health service. They cite the key players in the care of older people in order of significance as: older people themselves, those who care for them when necessary, social support and social care, community health services and medical care. Their conclusion is that one of the most underdeveloped components of clinical care for older people is multidisciplinary teams, particularly those working within public health community trusts. They also identify an essential component of future health planning, citing the importance of partnerships in care that support and develop the increasing role of non-medical staff. These in turn strengthen partnerships with secondary care, health authorities and social services within a framework of multidisciplinary education and training that encompasses patient and carer information and involvement.

Conclusions

Planning and recruitment to the study began in 1997, and 250 people have been assessed for fall risk, with appropriate referrals having been made. All have been reassessed at six, 12 and 18 months. Something that is very clear and will be reported upon fully in the near future is the enthusiasm, commitment and obvious pleasure demonstrated by the older people who have been assessed and who have attended the six-month programme. They have continued to meet regularly after the programme ended. The degree to which each individual component of the study will be transferred to an appropriate setting depends upon the analysis of the findings relating to the physiological and psychological changes of participants and to the rate at which they re-fall. The practical aspects of implementing the programme will contribute to many developments that are currently being considered by various health and social service providers.

Individuals and groups interested in the implementation of fall and fracture reduction projects or strategies are advised:
- to begin with a search for research findings relating to evidence of effectiveness;
- to process indicators which will provide essential information regarding collaboration between organizations who represent health, social services, local authorities and the voluntary sector;

- to collect expert statistical support in relation to data collection, which will inform the design, implementation and evaluation process of new developments;
- to gain local support from appropriate lead bodies, which might provide external support such as research and development funds, or from charities concerned with the ageing population.

The development of innovative preventative strategies in collaboration with primary care groups and trusts offers greater opportunities for encompassing primary and secondary care planning through health-promoting practice in a climate where public health working is crucial to its success.

References

Allen, A. and Simpson, J. M. (1999) A primary care based fall prevention programme, *Physiotherapy Theory and Practice*, 15(2): 57–144.

Arfken, C. L., Lach, H. W., Birge, S. J. and Miller, J. P. (1994) The prevalence and correlates of fear of falling in elderly persons living in the community, *American Journal of Public Health*, 84: 565–70.

Berg, W. P., Alessio, H. M., Mills, E. M. and Tong, C. (1997) Circumstances and consequences of falls in independent community-dwelling older adults, *Age and Ageing*, 26: 261–8.

Campbell, A. J., Borrie, M. J., Spears, G. F. *et al.* (1989) Circumstances and consequences of falls experienced by a community population 70 years and over during a prospective study, *Age and Ageing*, 19: 136–41.

Campbell, J., Robertson, C., Gardner, M. M., *et al.* (1997) Randomised controlled trial of a general practice programme of home based exercise to prevent falls in elderly women, *British Medical Journal*, 315: 1065–9.

Close, J. C., Ellis, M., Hooper, R. *et al.* (1999) Prevention of falls in the elderly trial (PROFET): a randomised controlled trial, *Lancet*, 353: 93–7.

Cooper, H., Ginn, J. and Arber, S. (1999) *Health-related Behaviour and Attitudes of Older People: A Secondary Analysis of National Datasets*. London: Health Education Authority.

Cottee, M. A. (1999) Recognising medical reasons for falling, *Physiotherapy Theory and Practice*, 15(2): 57–144.

Cryer, P. C. (1998) *Reducing Unintentional Injuries in Older People in England: Goals and Objectives for the Period 1998–2010*. London: South East Institute of Public Health.

Cryer, P. C., Davidson, L., Styles, C. P. and Langley, J. D. (1996) Descriptive epidemiology of injury in the South East: identifying priorities for action, *Public Health*, 110: 331–8.

Cummings, R. G., Miller, J. P., Kelsey, J. L. and Davis, P. (1991) Medications and multiple falls in elderly people: the St Louis OASIS study, *Age and Ageing*, 20: 455–61.

Dinan, S. and Sharp, C. (1996) *Fitness for Life*. London: Central YMCA.

Downton, J. H. (1993) *Falls in the Elderly*. London: Edward Arnold.

Dowswell, T., Towner, E., Cryer, C. *et al.* (1999) *Accidental Falls: Fatalities and Injuries. An Examination of the Data Sources and Review of the Literature on Preventive Strategies*. A report prepared for the Department of Trade and Industry. Newcastle upon Tyne and London: University of Newcastle and South East Institute of Public Health, University of London.

Duncan, P. W., Weiner, D. K., Chandler, J. and Studentski, S. (1990) Functional reach: a new clinical measure of balance, *Journal of Gerontology*, 45: M192–7.

Feder, G., Cryer, C. and Donovan, S. (1998) *Guidelines for the Prevention of Falls in Older*

People. London: Department of General Practice and Primary Care, Queen Mary and Westfield College London and South East Institute of Public Health.

Gaebler, S. (1993) Predicting which patient will fall again . . . and again, *Journal of Advanced Nursing*, 18: 1895–902.

Gibson, M. J., Andres, R. O., Isaacs, B., Radebaugh, T. and Worm-Peterson, J. (1987) The prevention of falls in later life. A report of the Kellogg International Work Group, *Danish Medical Bulletin*, 34: 1–24.

Health Education Authority (1998) *Older People in the Population*. Older People Fact Sheet 1. London: HEA.

Health Education Authority (1999) *Older People and Accidents*. Older People Fact Sheet 2. London: HEA.

Iliffe, S., Patterson, P. and Gould, M. M. (1998) *Health Care for Older People: Management in General Practice*. London: BMJ Books.

Iverson, B. D., Gossman, M. R., Shadeau, S. A. and Tucker, M. E. (1990) Balance performance, force production and activity levels in non-institutionalised men 60–90 years of age, *Physical Therapy*, 70: 348–55.

McMurdo, M. E. T. and Rennie, L. (1993) A controlled trial of exercise by residents of old people's homes, *Age and Ageing*, 22: 11–15.

Maki, B. E. and McIlroy, W. E. (1999) Control of compensatory stepping reactions: age-related impairment and the potential for remedial intervention, *Physiotherapy Theory and Practice*, 15(2): 57–144.

O'Loughlin, J. L., Robitaille, Y., Boivin, J-F. and Suissa, S. (1993) Incidence of risk factors for falls and injurious falls among the community-dwelling elderly, *American Journal of Epidemiology*, 137: 342–54.

Piotrowski Brown, A. (1999) Reducing falls in elderly people: a review of exercise interventions, *Physiotherapy Theory and Practice*, 15(2): 57–144.

Podsiadlo, D. and Richardson, S. (1991) The timed 'up and go': a test of basic functional mobility for frail elderly persons, *Journal of the American Geriatrics Society*, 39: 142–8.

Reece, A. C. and Simpson, J. M. (1996) Preparing older people to cope after a fall, *Physiotherapy*, 82: 227–35.

Secretary of State for Health (1999) *Saving Lives: Our Healthier Nation. A Contract for Health*. London: Stationery Office.

Simpson, J. M., Harrington, R. and Marsh, N. (1998) Guidelines for managing falls among elderly people, *Physiotherapy*, 84: 173–5.

Simpson, J. M. and Mandelstam, H. (1995) Elderly people at risk of falling: do they want to be taught how to get up again?, *Clinical Rehabilitation*, 9: 65–9.

Simpson, J. M. and Salkin, S. (1993) Are elderly people at risk of falling taught how to get up again?, *Age and Ageing*, 22: 294–6.

Skelton, D. A. and Dinan, S. M. (1999) Exercise for falls management: rationale for an exercise programme aimed at reducing postural instability, *Physiotherapy Theory and Practice*, 15(2): 57–144.

Skelton D. A. and McLaughlin A. W. (1996) Training functional ability in old age, *Physiotherapy*, 82: 159–67.

Snaith R. P. and Zigmond A. S. (1994) *The Hospital Anxiety and Depression Scale Manual*. Windsor: NFER-Nelson.

Sowden, A., Sheldon, T., Pehl, L. *et al.* (1996) *Effective Health Care Bulletin for Decision Makers on the Effectiveness of Health Service Interventions: Preventing Falls and Subsequent Injury in Older People*. Edinburgh: Churchill Livingstone.

Thomson, M. A. (1998) Closing the gap between nursing research and practice, *Evidence-based Nursing: Implementation Forum*, 1(1): 7–8.

Tinetti, M. E. (1994) Prevention of falls and fall injuries in elderly persons: a research agenda, *Preventive Medicine*, 23: 756–62.

Tinetti, M. E., Baker, D. I., McAvay, G. *et al.* (1994) A multifactorial intervention to reduce the risk of falling among elderly people living in the community, *New England Journal of Medicine*, 331: 821–7.

Tinetti, M. E., Richman, D. and Powell, L. (1990) Falls efficacy as a measure of fear of falling, *Journal of Gerontology*, 45: 239–43.

Tinetti, M. E., Speechley, M. and Ginter, F. (1988) Risk factors for falls among elderly persons living in the community, *New England Journal of Medicine*, 319: 1701–7.

Tinetti, M. E., Wen-Liang, L. and Claus, B. (1993) Predictors and prognosis of inability to get up after falls among elderly persons, *Journal of the American Medical Association*, 269: 65–70.

Tones, K. and Tilford, S. (1994) *Health Education: Effectiveness, Efficacy and Equity.* London: Chapman and Hall.

Vandervoort, A. A. (1999) Ankle mobility and postural stability, *Physiotherapy Theory and Practice*, 15(2): 57–144.

Vellas, B. J., Wayne, S. J., Romero, L. J., Baumgartner, R. N. and Garry, P. J. (1997) Fear of falling and restriction of mobility in elderly fallers, *Age and Ageing*, 26: 189–93.

Wagner, E. H., LaCroix, A. Z., Grothaus, L. *et al.* (1994) Preventing disability and falls in older adults: a population-based randomized trial, *American Journal of Public Health*, 84: 1800–6.

Webb, P. (ed.) (1994) *Enhancing Health and Function in Later Life: Health Promotion and Patient Education.* London: Chapman and Hall.

Zigmond, A. S. and Snaith, R. P. (1983) The Hospital Anxiety and Depression Scale, *Acta Psychiatrica Scandinavica*, 67: 361–70.

9

Understanding and working with grief and loss

— PATRICIA HAYMAN AND NERYS JAMES —

For life and death are one,
even as the river and the sea are one.

The Prophet

This chapter explores the notion of attachment, bereavement and grief. Two theoretical models documented by Parkes and Worden are used to further understanding of the grief process. Common reactions to grief are outlined and linked to Rogers's person-centred model of working and to other holistic strategies. There is a need to understand the process of grief and loss and to find ways of staying and working with strong feelings which are a part of the natural response to loss. We attempt to share with the reader what we have learned.

Before one can fully comprehend the impact of loss and its associated human behaviour, it is important to have some understanding of the meaning of attachment. There is considerable writing in the psychological literature as to the nature of attachments, what they are and how they develop. One of the key figures and primary thinkers in this area was the British psychiatrist John Bowlby. His publication of *Attachment and Loss* (1969) proved to be a turning point in the history of psychoanalysis and psychology. It is Bowlby's assertion that loss throws us back to profoundly disturbing separation anxiety that we experienced as children. Bowlby's attachment theory provides a way for us to conceptualize the tendency in human beings to make strong affectional bonds with others, and provides a way to understand the strong emotional reaction that occurs when those bonds are threatened or broken. Bowlby's thesis is that attachments come from a need for security and safety. Through experiments he demonstrated that human attachment is an instinctive response to the need for protection against predators and is as important for survival as nutrition and reproduction. These attachments develop early in life, and are usually directed towards a few significant individuals, and tend to endure throughout the life cycle. Loss and separation experienced as babies and children may not be remembered, but form part of the inner emotional world. If the comfort received was enough to help the baby to manage the separation, resources would be formed and strengthened and a step towards independence gained. This legacy of self-awareness can then be accessed as adults facing separation and loss. Bowlby's theory is that it is the quality of early attachments that may affect and influence our ability today to cope with loss.

Stroebe *et al.* (1993: 5) define bereavement as 'the objective situation of having lost someone significant', and mourning as 'the manner of expressing grief which can be influenced by our culture'. Bereavement requires us to make a transition of change. Transition can be viewed, as a period of change, growth and disequilibrium that serves as a kind of bridge between one relatively stable point in life and another relatively stable but different point. Bereavement and loss in particular require that we revise all our internal assumptions, expectations, the view of ourselves and the world around us. The world is no longer as it should be. It may feel as if it has collapsed, it is disorganized. Everyday basic tasks to function, cope and survive may have been tied up with that which is now lost, and therefore these tasks seem pointless. This inner experience and preoccupation may interfere with the ability to adapt to what has happened. Gradually, reintegration takes place as mourning progresses, and the bonds to the attached lost object are gradually undone, separated and reinvested in life and living again. Because our internal constructs are individual and unique, so the process of grief is individual and unique.

Worden (1983) states that mourning is necessary and that certain tasks must be accomplished for equilibrium to be established and the process of mourning complete. For grief to be resolved, Worden suggests, there are four different aspects to be addressed: emotional, physical, behavioural and cognitive. Worden's tasks are as follows:

1 To accept the reality of the loss.
2 To work through the pain of grief.
3 To adjust to an environment in which the deceased is missing.
4 To relocate the deceased emotionally and move on with life.

Murray Parkes (1972) defines the grief process in stages:

1 Numbness, confusion, disorganization; reality of the loss takes time.
2 Yearning and searching for the lost object. Anger and guilt.
3 Mitigation, no sense of purpose and continuous attempts to make sense of the loss. What is left is meaningless and purposeless.
4 The final stage of the process is to gain a new identity. A 'widow is no longer a wife, she is a widow' (Murray Parkes 1972: 111). Unexpectedly, we have become I. The process of giving up the old identity and forming a new one can be a long and painful process.

To understand the grief process it is important to recognize that whatever model is used, the bereaved or those facing loss and change may visit and revisit the different aspects of their grief, moving in and out of the tasks or phases helping them to cope with the transition of change. In so doing they are seeking a way of making some sense of their loss by reviewing and rebuilding their internal world in order to cope and adjust to change. With these models in mind it is important to consider these tasks and phases, as they incorporate the common reactions to grief. Emotional suffering evokes strong feelings.

Emotional suffering

Shock

For the bereaved it may feel as if a veil has been drawn between themselves and the outside world, a feeling of being on the outside looking in, a sense of bewilderment. This is often coupled with physical symptoms, such as numbness, coldness, loss of appetite, dry throat, difficulty in swallowing, breathlessness and fainting.

Denial

Denial is a psychological unconscious defence that protects us from overwhelming feelings and pain until we are ready to deal with reality. Denial can last for moments or for years. It is unhealthy for denial to last for long periods of time as it can contribute to unresolved grief. It can prolong, postpone or even inhibit grieving. Denial can be used to protect and separate from frightening feelings, and may create blocks in the grief process, thus storing up difficulties and complications for the future. Grief may appear to disappear, but it lies dormant underground and creates a block to resolution. Parkes's research suggests that when a person doesn't have enough external or internal support or the internal resources to cope with loss, acceptance and breaking through denial can be difficult. Worden states that the bereaved need to accept the death of a significant person on an intellectual and emotional level.

Anger

When a loved one dies, they become the lost object – our powerlessness to locate them causes anger. Who can the anger be diverted at? The deceased? Doctors? God? Nurses? Care workers? Anger with oneself and thoughts of 'if only' can lead to feelings of guilt and the angry question, 'Why me? It is all part of the grief felt when a loved one is lost; it is a natural and healthy response to a painful loss.

Anger is frequently experienced after loss and can come from two sources, a sense of frustration and a regressive experience that occurs after the loss of someone close who has died. Worden (1983: 15) based on work by Horowitz *et al.* (1980), suggests that 'Bereavement can lead to intense regression where the bereaved perceive themselves as helpless, inadequate, incapable, childlike, or personally bankrupt.' Angry feelings stem from the intense pain that is being experienced, and failure to express anger may result in the anger being turned against the self, leading to depression. Anger can be expressed as resentment, hatred, envy and a sense of unfairness.

Guilt

Guilt can descend and strangle rational thought, but helpers can challenge the guilt and invariably it will yield itself to reality testing. Talking about our assumed failures and neglect can give a sense of realistic proportion to guilt and lead to self-forgiveness. The 'if onlys' can be so guilt-laden and endless, especially if the death was unnatural. Clients can torment themselves and suffer anguish over things they wished they had said or done. Guilt is often the result of anger.

Sorrow and despair

At a time of the most intense sadness, the impact of reality begins to set in as clients struggle to come to terms with what they have lost. Sometimes the losses take time to be realized. If it is a partner, some of those losses may include loss of role and identity that might have been intertwined in their partner, loss of lover, friend, gardener, loss of status. Reduction of income may create further loss and stress.

Perhaps it is the loss of their dreams, loss of expectation and an assumption of sharing their future with the significant one that is lost. Anguish may be experienced as all that was tied up and invested in the lost one now feels fruitless and barren. Emotional pain can obliterate all sense of belonging, sometimes leading to a feeling of the loss of the self. Murray Parkes (1972) describes the feeling of meaninglessness and purposelessness after bereavement. 'The pain of grief can feel like shattered glass, splinters in the heart that empathy, understanding and acceptance can remove' (Hayman 1994). The cognitive/behavioural response to the grief process may be a sense of disorganization, confusion and disorientation. This can feed into the helplessness and powerlessness that may be experienced. The usual cognitive capacities may take a battering from the onslaught and myriad of feelings, leaving those who always considered themselves emotionally strong feeling overwhelmed.

Acceptance

Worden (1983), quoting Bowlby and Colin Murray Parkes, states that mourning is finished when a person completes the final mourning stage of restitution. There is a reinvestment in other relationships, and an ability to talk about the deceased without being overwhelmed with pain. A sense of sadness may always remain. The tides of the sea ebb and flow, just as grief will ebb and flow. Grief rushes in and threatens to overwhelm again, and then leaves in quietness, before the next significant date. These dates come and go, and matter because the feelings about them matter. That is the nature of grief, the nature of the sea and its ebb and flow.

Colours of Grief

The colour of grief is black, layer upon layer, it covers me whole;
the weight and burden a heavy load,
I cannot lift my head out of its depths, no light at the end of the road.

The colour of my pain is purple, bloods flowing purple
and I bleed, how I bleed.
Hold me tight with the colour of compassion and love.
So many tears do fall, crystal clear in their colourless light.
The colour of my anger is red; stark bright blinding sight
my heart reeling in its excess, lay your hands upon me still,
whisper, let it go, let it go.
The colour of my loneliness is grey, grey walls, grey skies,
grey upon grey, no relief to the grey relentless void into which I fall.
The colour of acceptance is blue, soft like your skin, so smooth, so cool.
Wrap me in blue lightness, wash away, blacks, greys and purples,
Lift me to the sky to bathe me in blue; it's time to say goodbye to you,
but I loved you, Oh, how I loved you.

(Hayman 1994)

Working with loss

It is important at this stage to note that grief is a natural process. It is only
when someone gets stuck in this process and fails to move on, reinvesting in
life, that it becomes unhealthy, resulting in unresolved or pathological grief.
This natural process is influenced by society, culture and family traditions and
patterns. 'All the major religions of the world teach that there is some sort of
continuity or survival after death' (Firth 1989: 254). This can offer hope and
comfort to some facing loss through bereavement and assist in making sense
of what they are experiencing. Different religions and cultures can provide a
framework or markers for mourners aiding the process of mourning. Bowlby
asserts: 'In these ways a culture channels the psychological responses of individuals and in some degree ritualises them. The origins of the responses themselves lie, however, at a deeper level' (in Lendrum and Syme 1992: 48).
However, in our Western death-denying society today, these rituals have
almost disappeared, probably adding to the mourners' difficulty in finding
some direction in their grief process, as they receive little acknowledgment of
their loss from society. All these factors need to be held in our awareness
when we work with people facing grief, loss and significant change.

The older person may have to contend with the multiple griefs of growing
old. These griefs may include some of the following: loss of vision, hearing,
loss of mobility through arthritis, respiratory or cardiac disease, loss of health
and well-being, loss of sexual function. Loss of brain function can be subtle,
with minimal losses allied with ageing. It can be more progressive and
destructive (Raphael 1984). The more mobility and independence are affected,
the greater the sense of loss, producing more intense grief reactions and thus
the need to make a psychosocial transition (Murray Parkes 1972). Some of
these losses, if anticipated and prepared for, may not be as intense. As older
people realize they cannot do as much as they used to, there is the need to
recognize their own death and acknowledge the loss of unfulfilled hopes and
dreams. 'Nevertheless many older people, especially those who are physically
well and have a confidant, have a high level of psychological well being'

(Larson 1978: 296). With ageing there is sometimes less social contact, and loneliness and isolation are frequent complaints (Raphael 1984: 307). Time may be spent mourning relationships that are now lost; the sad, happy, good and bad times need to be reflected upon. There will be sorrow that they are no more. There are specific considerations regarding grief and mourning for the older person. In long-term relationships day-to-day ritual is safe, secure and familiar. There may be greater mutual dependence, particularly where there is ill-health with a spouse. Socialization may diminish, there may be more focus on children and grandchildren. Work may have been relinquished. The need for a partner will be great, despite any ambivalence. Death may be rehearsed between the couple, including what they will do if the other goes first. Some anticipatory grief work may be done prior to the death of a partner. The frequent expression may be 'What will I do without him/her?' This underlies a sense of helplessness and aloneness and fear of the future. Rapheal (1984) cites Shulman (1978) concerning the higher risk of para-suicide and suicide in old age. Recent bereavement heightens the risk. Loss of a spouse following a long relationship may deny the surviving partner the remaining source of physical and emotional closeness and the comfort of being of worth and value as an individual. If the deceased was the carer the fear for the survivor is even greater. Women often see themselves as surviving better than men. Their knowledge and basic housekeeping skills enable them to cope more effectively. The younger bereaved may have a clearer picture of their future, but for the older person, when his or her spouse dies, that view of the future diminishes. The surviving spouse may hold on to the image of his or her partner, lessening the need to grieve and mourn (Raphael 1984).

The core conditions of person-centred counselling (Rogers 1959) can incorporate a way of working holistically to promote health for the older person. What did Rogers mean by person-centred counselling? Rogers (1959) stated that individuals have within themselves vast resources for self-understanding and for altering their self-concepts, basic attitudes and self-directed behaviour. These core conditions can be used in any setting where the worker wishes to help the patient or client to accept the reality of grief, loss or change. Rogers believed that every individual has the potential for growth when provided with the correct core conditions of congruence, unconditional positive regard and empathy. Mearns and Thorne (1988: 74, 54, 39) define the core conditions as follows: 'congruence is the state of being of the counsellor when her outward responses to her client consistently match the inner feelings and sensations which she has in relation to the client . . . Unconditional positive regard is the label given to the fundamental attitude of the person centered counsellor towards her client. The counsellor who holds this attitude deeply values the humanity of her client and is not deflected in that valuing by any particular client behaviours. The attitude manifests itself in the counsellor's consistent acceptance and enduring warmth towards her client . . . Empathy is a continuing process whereby the counsellor lays aside her own way of experiencing and perceiving reality, preferring to sense and to respond to the experiences and perceptions of the client. So congruency is a state of being in relation to the client, empathy is a process and unconditional positive regard is an attitude. To offer core conditions is to offer warmth, acceptance and understanding, which Rogers believed provided the climate to assist change. What can professional helpers, carers and counsellors offer those facing bereavement, loss and change? They can offer hope, change and growth within the relationship they share with clients, a relationship that is warm, accepting, holding, consistent and non-judgemental. They can help them to make sense of their loss and in so doing review and rebuild their internal world in order to cope and adjust to change.

Supportive holistic strategies

> You give but little when you give of your possessions. It is when you give of yourself that you truly give.
>
> *The Prophet*

There are some dos and don'ts in this area. The dos are:

- Be yourself and relate in a genuine manner.
- Listen in an active concentrated way, watching for verbal and non-verbal cues.
- Listen to what but more importantly how something is said. Listen for the feelings and emotions behind the words.
- Facilitate clients need to talk about their loss and grief. This helps clients to receive undivided attention and not feel a burden to the listener. It helps them to have their difficult feelings recognized and understood (Lendrum and Syme 1992).
- Allow a sharing of the happy and sad times, which are being missed. This is an important part of working through the process and making sense of the loss.
- Acknowledge their feelings. The bereaved are so often faced with avoidance, creating further isolation. Often words are unnecessary.

The don'ts are:

- Don't say 'it's all right', when clearly it is not.
- Try to avoid changing the subject or telling them what they should do, think or feel.
- Don't express or indicate that they should be over their loss or have adapted to the change by now. Each individual has his or her own time scale and grief in particular takes as long as it takes.
- Do not judge.
- Don't say 'I know how you feel' because we cannot know how that person is feeling even if we have had similar experiences.

This links to an important issue of self-awareness. Benjamin Franklin stated that there are three things that are extremely hard: steel, a diamond and to know one's self. Without this knowledge it may be difficult to handle strong emotions in others and the emotions that may be evoked in us if we haven't come to terms with our own previous losses or significant changes. This awareness helps to separate our own issues from those of the client, thus protecting the client and ourselves. Personal limitations need to be recognized and emotional support sought when necessary. Failure to do so could lead to stress. Personal crisis in our own lives enables us to learn that our own vulnerability and pain, when handled with support and supervision, increases our ability to reach out and extend a helping hand to others. Out of our suffering, strength and growth follow, enabling us to help and support our clients along their road of crisis. Helpful responses foster growth and heal the wounds of grief. We know that any one loss may evoke feelings from previous losses. Unhelpful responses devalue. Our role as helpers is therefore to accept, be congruent, be empathic without wishing to change the client's experience in any way that perhaps makes us more comfortable.

We recognize that knowledge, understanding and self-awareness need to be an important foundation to a holistic approach to working with the bereaved or clients who have experienced a major loss. It is a journey and that journey is enriching for both client and helper as they work towards healing and acceptance.

References

Bowlby, J. (1969) *Attachment and Loss*. London: Pimlico.

Dickenson, D. and Johnson, M. (eds) (1993) *Death, Dying and Bereavement*. Buckingham: Open University Press.

Firth, D. (1989) *Nursing the Dying*. London: Tavistock/Routledge.

Gibran, K. (1926) *The Prophet*. London, Heinemann.

Hayman, P. (1994) *Legacy of Suicide*. Seminar proceedings, Weybridge, Silverlands, 11 November.

Hayman, P. (1996) Colours of grief, in Hourihan, M. (ed.) *Light of the World*. Exeter: Wheatons.

Holmes, J. (1993) *John Bowlby and Attachment Theory*. London: Routledge.

Horowitz, M. J., Wilner, N., Marmar, C., and Krupuik, J. (1980) Pathological grief and the activation of latent self images, *American Journal of Psychiatry*, 137: 1157–62.

Larson, R. (1978) Thirty years of research on subjective wellbeing of older Americans, *Journal of Gerontology*, 33: 109–25.

Lendrum, S. and Syme, G. (1992) *Gift of Tears*. London: Routledge.

Mearns, D. and Thorn, B. (1998) *Person Centered Counselling in Action*. London: Sage.

Murray Parkes, C. (1972) *Bereavement. Studies of Grief in Adult Life*. London: Penguin.

Raphael, B. (1984) *The Anatomy of Bereavement*. London: Unwin Hyman.

Rogers, C. (1959) *Person Centred Counselling in Action*. London: Sage.

Shulman, K. (1978) Suicide and parasuicide in old age: a review, *Age and Aging*, 7: 210–29.

Stroebe, M. S., Stroebe., R. and Hansson, R. O. (eds) (1993) *Handbook of Bereavement. Theory, Research, and Intervention*. Cambridge: Cambridge University Press.

Worden, J. W. (1983) *Grief Counselling and Grief Therapy*. London: Routledge.

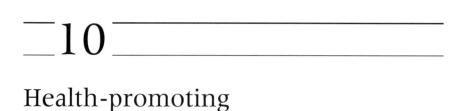

10

Health-promoting
residential settings

___ ANNE SQUIRE ___

This chapter examines and questions key concepts about health promotion in residential settings. It suggests that these settings can offer a worthwhile and justifiable approach to health care for the older person, which can maintain and promote health and well-being to improve the quality of life of the residents. It describes relevant theories and models, within the context of stated aims such as those of the United Nations International Year of the Older Person. I consider the concept of the settings approach and the underlying assumptions in a residential environment. Finally, the chapter introduces the ethical and moral issues surrounding health-promoting residential settings to encourage the reader to reflect on his or her own role in health care with the older person.

The United Nations (UN) International Year of Older Persons (United Nations European Resource Unit UK 1999) identified four central issues for the year 1999 and the future:

- the situation of older people;
- lifelong individual development;
- multigenerational relationships;
- relationships between population ageing and development.

The UN's International Plan of Action for Older People focuses on the situation of older people in terms of:

- independence;
- participation;
- care;
- self-fulfilment;
- dignity.

These key issues emphasize the need to embrace the following fundamentals:

- Does an older person really need residential care?
- The type of health promotion and care carried out in residential settings today and in future.
- Do residential care staff foster a health promoting environment or setting for the residents?
- How is the physical, mental, social, emotional and spiritual health of the older person's individual development encouraged?
- Are multigenerational relationships promoted?
- What is the relationship between the ageing population and society?

Residential settings

To avoid confusion, we need to look at what we are referring to as residential settings. In this chapter they are residential homes, nursing homes, long-stay care in hospitals and sheltered housing.

Victor (1995) contends that the image of later life is often one of seeing our days out in residential care and institutionalization. She argues that the percentage of older people living in institutional environments does increase with age, but more older people live in the community. Is this why residential settings are not usually included in health promotion strategic planning and organization, or is it more an ageist approach?

Settings were described as a concept in the Health of the Nation strategy (1992). Health promotion activities are usually described in relation to different settings, such as the workplace, cities, schools, hospitals and primary health care, but not residential settings. Interventions with target groups for health promotion sometimes include older people but, unfortunately, generally only within their own homes or the community. It can be said that the residential setting is within a community but, in reality, health promotion departments organize their activities with older people living in their own homes or with relatives and friends. Is this because of the negative connotations of residential care (Nolan *et al.* 1996)? Allen *et al.* (1992) point out that older people and their carers do not relish the idea of institutional care. Why is this? What kind of a picture do we have of residential settings? Is it one of frail older people who have lost their physical independence and dignity? The end of the line?

What is health promotion?

We need to define health promotion in a residential setting. The World Health Organization (WHO) (1987) defines it as the process of enabling people to increase control over, and to improve, their health. This fits favourably with the concept of older people in residential settings and the UN focus. It is about fostering and maintaining positive health, not just preventing disease. Ewles and Simnett (1999) suggest that health promotion is raising the health status of individuals and communities. Health education, or education for health as the WHO now calls it, is necessary in all health promotion programmes. Health promotion is an umbrella expression for a variety of policy developments, which include health education (Tones *et al.* 1991).

Health promotion theories and models

Tones *et al.* (1991) state that there is clear evidence that human behaviour is amenable to change. Health promotion models have been organized into different approaches or typologies. Health promoters should work with one or more models to clarify their aims and values, so that they can assess, plan, implement and evaluate their health promotion programmes. Rambo (1984) emphasizes the value of using models in the assessment process because they provide a systematic approach and pointers to potential problems and solutions. Different elements of each model can be incorporated into the programme, be it a one-off, opportunistic teaching session or a long-term health promotion programme. This is necessary when carrying out health promotion for older people, because of their diverse interests and life experiences. It will also help the health promoter to think of new ways of working and new proposals for care. Schober (1989) argues that models help to make sense of the range of alternatives available to health promoters by providing an infrastructure around which a package of care can be individually tailored and developed to meet a client's needs. Ewles and Simnett (1999) identify a framework of five approaches to health promotion.

The medical or preventive approach

This approach focuses on disease, disability and the medicalization of life. Health promoters in residential settings endeavour to increase medical interventions which would prevent or improve ill-health. For example, the immunization of older people to prevent influenza and screening for osteoporosis could be seen as a medical approach. This technique values preventive medical procedures and has high prestige because of its epidemiological background. It is often seen as paternalistic because of the persuasive, expert-led, top-down and compliance methods that it uses. As we can see, there are advantages and disadvantages to this approach but as long as we use it with the unmitigated consent of older people, it is a suitable process for a residential setting.

The behaviour change approach

This approach seeks to improve older people's health by changing their behaviour and attitudes. It encourages and persuades them to adopt a healthy lifestyle. It assumes that, if information about risk factors is given to them, by one-to-one advice or mass campaigns, they will adjust their behaviour to avoid or minimize the risks. There is a belief in this model that people make rational decisions and are responsible for their own health and social care. According to Naidoo and Wills (1995), this approach is well liked because it views health as the property of individuals. Examples are teaching older people to be more physically active and eat a healthy diet. It can be used in residential care but, unfortunately, a constant finding in the evaluation of this method is that merely changing knowledge does not necessarily lead to behaviour change. Weinstein (1994) suggested links between people's

perception of the severity of the outcome of an illness and their percept
the risk of personal susceptibility to an illness. He developed a model c.
the Precaution Adoption Model, which has five stages through which peo
pass:

- lack of awareness of an issue;
- becoming aware and personally engaged;
- engaged and taking active decisions about what to do;
- planning to act;
- finally acting.

This model is useful in clarifying why knowledge only estimates elements in
the process of behaviour change but may be unlinked to the final behaviour
change. The important concept to remember is the need to consider the older
person's readiness to change (Prochaska and DiClemente 1984). Ebrahim and
Davey Smith (1996) argue that older people need information on the effects
of lifestyle modification because they have not had the advantage of health
promotion when they were at school or in early adult life.

The educational approach

This approach aims to provide heath education in terms of giving information
for older people to gain knowledge, either on an individual basis or in group
educational programmes. It is expected that they will be able to make well
informed decisions about their health and social well-being. The educational
approach differs from the behaviour change approach in that it does not insti-
gate change in any particular direction. It does not persuade or motivate
people to change but allows them to make an informed choice about their
health and well-being. Access to information is one way to vindicate the
impact of ageism. Giving information about what can contribute, for example,
to good mental health, helps older people to become more aware of their
ability to optimize their own health. In a residential setting equipping older
people with knowledge can help them to share and explore their attitudes to
their own health.

Societal change approach

This approach aims to influence changes in the physical, social and economic
environment for older people on a small or a large scale. This could be through
putting the concept of 'home' for older people on the political agenda at all
levels, locally and nationally. Do we have 'health promoting homes' that older
people want to go into? Do we ask older people what they want and act on
their comments? The Millennium Debate of the Age was seen as a crucial
challenge for the end of the twentieth century in how we plan to manage our
society when there will be fewer young people and many more older ones.
This may require major social changes in how we want to live in the future.
The Debate of the Age is the largest independent pubic consultation ever
undertaken by the government.

The client-centred approach or the empowerment model

This aims to work with older people on their own terms, the main health promotion activity being to empower them. Given the importance of empowerment for people as they get older, and the need to challenge ageism, I now debate the concept of empowerment.

Empowerment of older people

One of the major elements of health promotion is the concept of empowerment of people. Empowerment is an area that deserves special attention when addressing older people in residential settings. The concept of empowerment is diverse and eludes a single definition. According to Naidoo and Wills (1998), empowering people is ensuring they help determine the way their health is to be promoted and acknowledging the value of their perspective. It is about helping people to acquire the skills and self-assurance to take greater control of their lives and their health, which includes the ability to take effective action on your own behalf. Tones and Tilford (1994) describe empowerment as central to the ideology and practice of heath promotion. They discuss the notion of community empowerment and empowerment of the individual, which they call self-empowerment. Strategies can extend from the provision of information about a particular service to democratic control of decision-making bodies.

Tones (1993) suggests that there are four elements to empowerment:

- the environmental situation which may either assist the exercise of control or present a barrier to independent action;
- the degree to which individuals actually have competencies or skills which facilitate them to control some aspects of their lives and conquer environmental barriers;
- the degree to which individuals believe they are in control of their own lives and health;
- numerous emotional conditions or traits which frequently accompany different beliefs about control, e.g. older people not feeling valued, feeling helpless, unloved, not needed by society, family and friends, suffering from depression, poor self-esteem or feelings of self-worth.

Langer's and Rodin's (1976) field experiment shows the use of a societal, behavioural and an empowerment approach when they looked at the independence and personal control of a group of older people in a modern high-quality nursing home. In the home, two floors were selected because of the equivalence in the residents' physical and psychological health, the length of time in the home and their prior socio-economic status. Rather than subjects being randomly assigned to experimental treatment, a different floor was randomly selected for each treatment. In the 'responsibility-induced' experimental group, residents were given a communication emphasizing their responsibility for themselves. There were many opportunities for change, such as the way the home was run, and they were given the freedom to make choices. Instead of the staff making changes, the experimental group were asked what changes they would like to make. They were invited to dete how the furniture in their rooms should be arranged and were given va plants to be responsible for. The communication given to the compar. group stressed the staff's responsibility for the older people. The comparis group, who lived on a different but comparable floor in the home, were given plants which were looked after by the staff. They were not invited to make any changes to their rooms or the environment. The difference between the two groups was that on one floor residents were responsible for themselves, on the other floor the staff were responsible for the residents. Before an investigation into whether or not the experimental treatment was successful, the pre-test ratings made by the interviewer, subjects and the staff were compared for both groups. None of the differences approached significance, which indicated comparability between the groups preceding the start of the investigation. Eighteen months later, questionnaire ratings and behavioural measures showed a significant improvement for the experimental group over the comparison group. Measures of activity level and general happiness were noted. There was a significant difference in the quality of life of the empowered experimental group. The empowered 'responsibility-induced' group were more contented than the comparison group, in that they were happier, exhibited active participation, were alert, felt valued and had a greater sense of belonging whereas, in the comparison group, 71 per cent were rated as 'having become more debilitated'. In contrast, 93 per cent of the empowered experimental group actually showed 'overall improvement'. This significant social change show us how important it is to focus at the policy and environmental level. The results clearly shows us the importance of empowerment and allowing older people to have responsibility for their own life style.

The importance of empowerment before and after going into a residential setting seems clear. Older people need support to be autonomous and to be able to participate in their choice of whether or not to go into residential care, the choice of where to go and what type of care they get. According to Doyal and Gough (1991), autonomy is one of the basic human needs: interestingly, they cite the other as physical health. Like Tones, they consider that autonomy and empowerment is being able 'to make informed choices about what should be done and how to go about it'. Sinclair (1988) points out that older people rarely make the decision to enter residential settings. Care is usually organized because of a crisis such as being discharged from hospital and being unable to cope. Nolan and Caldock (1996) identify the problem of the choice of setting: often the older person is too ill or too frail to take part in the decision, and usually no forward planning has been carried out to decide what should happen if the older person is unable to continue to live at home. This is often because of the fear of institutionalized care. Older people should have their fundamental needs for autonomy and empowerment met so that they can participate in their chosen lifestyle. This requires the provision of health-promoting environments in the community and in residential settings. Statutory and voluntary bodies must be responsible for providing care that older people can choose for themselves, having a positive view of the health of older people and accepting them as partners in promoting and maintaining their health care. Empowerment and autonomy can still work along with interdependence – how we live together, support one another – respecting older people's values and beliefs and helping them to make their choices of care.

What promotes and maintains older people's health in a residential setting?

A combination of different measures seem to be important, such as the promotion of physical, social, emotional, mental and spiritual health. This could include:

- a 'homely' environment, flowers, colourful crockery, tablecloths;
- recreational activities;
- social activities and social support;
- promoting physical activity;
- health check-ups;
- healthy eating, relaxed meal times, food as something to look forward to, good nutrition, with individual diets chosen by themselves;
- individual care for the very frail elderly;
- help and advice on smoking cessation;
- moderation in alcohol consumption;
- privacy;
- improving self-awareness, self-esteem and decision-making;
- sexual health;
- rest, sleep and relaxation;
- interpersonal relationships, good communication, listening, giving time for the older person, tone of voice, touch, respect and empathy;
- opportunities to reflect, to listen, to be calm and tranquil and to relax or meditate;
- encouragement and guidance to come to terms with their lives, helping them to have a sense of identity, and promoting their self-esteem;
- time to reflect and discuss their cultural roots, their understanding of a spiritual quest with the person of their choice, such as a priest;
- opportunities for prayer in the environment of their choice, such as membership of a church;
- welcoming all family members, carers, friends and family pets;
- encouraging personal relationships, autonomy and empowerment;
- preventing diseases and problems that are common as we get older, such as accidents and injury prevention, cancer, cardiovascular disease, heart disease, stroke, diabetes, osteoporosis, eyesight and hearing health promotion, promoting foot health, continence advice and support, oral and dental health promotion.

Health promotion and health education activities

Older people are targeted in the European Union's health promotion policy (WHO 1993), but the *Health of the Nation* document (Secretary of State for Health 1992) highlights reducing 'premature death' and identifies upper age limits for health targets. This seems to imply that good health is more important for younger people than for older people. Surely this is an ageist policy?

Health education for older people is not new. There are many excellent programmes being carried out in the community, such as Ageing Well, Adding Life to Years, leisure centre activities, aerobics and tea dances. Older people are now being asked what kind of programmes they would like in the community, although most are for the fitter, more mobile older person. How do residents fit into this scenario? How often do they go out of the home to join in with these activities? How often do health promoters – that is, all concerned with health and social care – see older people in residential care and invite them to activities such as walks, exercise classes or aqua mobile classes? Are they not part of the community because they are not living in their own homes? Staff in residential settings are being asked what kind of education and training they need by voluntary bodies such as British Association for Service to the Elderly (BASE). Although many topic areas are requested for education and training, most residential care staff do not ask for health promotion topics (author's experience and data collected by BASE). Is this because they think older people don't need it? Is ageism endemic? Or is it because they don't understand the concept of health promotion and older people? It seems self-evident that, if health promotion interventions are to be successful in residential settings, it is essential that staff understand health promotion theories and models, though much more is needed, such as a change in society's knowledge about and attitudes to the older person. We must start to talk and listen to all older people, valuing their knowledge and skills. It is time to stop referring to the 'burden' of the growing numbers of older people but to ask what we can learn from them.

The health promotion residential environment

Reflecting on the UN's focus and Tones's four elements of empowerment, let us consider what a health-promoting environment is. Wallace (1994) argues that, although there is confirmation of variations in health according to the vicinity of residence, less research has been focused on how the quality of the local environment may affect the health of older people. Tones (1993) believes that if we disregard the significance of an unfavourable environment on health and illness we will be guilty of 'victim blaming'; in other words, trying to get older people to 'fit into' the residential environment, instead of making the environment a healthier and happy place to live in, then 'blaming the victims' for their own ill-health. What do older people want from residential care? Do they want a health promoting environment?

Counsel and Care (1992) interviewed people attending day centres and groups of residents in private and voluntary homes about what they wished to see in residential care homes. The researchers found that the older people not living in a residential setting wanted the following:

- no restrictions on going out;
- transport;
- social and leisure activities;
- visits from family and friends;
- kindness and respect;

- privacy, a room of their own;
- their own furniture;
- control of their own finances.

These examples are not surprising, as we all want to live our lives without controls, to make our own choices, to be free to do what we like whenever possible. All too often, in dealings with older people, their right to retain control over their lives is overlooked. We are all social beings who need the company of people of our own choice. We need people to respect our rights, the right to determine our own lives and to expect quality in the care we are given. Most people need their private space to be able to reflect mentally and emotionally.

The older people living in residential care offered the following:

- privacy, to be able to lock their room door;
- an en-suite bathroom;
- an alternative sitting room;
- choice of meals and advance menus;
- to get up when they wish;
- to be treated as friends not patients.

There are important issues here. The Counsel and Care research found that most of the above were not being addressed, and the residential settings were not health-promoting environments. Their findings show a lack of privacy and choices, inadequacy in social contact and suitable activities to stimulate the body and mind and the deprivation of the fundamental right of older people to be seen as equals. All concerned need awareness of the ethical issues underpinning our actions. The following 'adapted' set of questions developed by Ewles and Simnett (1999) is useful to question our basic principles and standards.

1 Questions fundamental to decisions about the health of older people. Do I:
   - Create autonomy for older people?
   - Respect the autonomy of older people, whether or not I approve of what they are doing?
   - Respect older people equally, without discrimination?
2 Questions about duties and principles. Do I:
   - Do good and prevent harm?
   - Tell the truth?
   - Minimize harm in the long term?
   - Honour promises and agreements?
3 Questions about consequences. Do I:
   - Increase individual good or act for the good of myself?
   - Increase the good of older people?
   - Increase the social good for older people?
4 Questions about external considerations.
   - Am I putting resources to best use?
   - Is a degree of risk involved?
   - Is there a code of practice concerning this?
   - How certain am I of the facts; are they disputed?

- Are there legal implications, do I understand them?
- What are the views of the older person, families and carers?
- Can I justify my actions in terms of the evidence I have before me?

At whatever level we promote health, we should be asking ourselves these questions, to help us to think clearly and to deliberate about the ethical and moral issues surrounding health promotion. One way is for the owners, staff and residents to get together and look at what they think is good quality practice in health promotion and care. Moral and ethical dilemmas could be discussed and acted upon (as a team) by using the National Occupational Standards (NOS) in Health Promotion and Care. NOS are an important strategic and operational tool for organizations and individuals in residential settings (Care Sector Consortium 1997). They describe, for example, the performance required to deliver high-quality care in needs assessment and care planning, enabling people to manage change and disability and promoting health and social well-being working in partnership with clients, professionals and agencies.

Owners, staff and residents can use the standards as a reference to describe and discuss what they are achieving and hope to achieve when living or working in a residential setting. NOS help people to make agreements about what they and their organization are accomplishing and are intending to accomplish, and to put those agreements into action in an understandable and knowledgeable way. Standards can help owners and staff to reflect on their practice. They also help residents to explore what type of a home they want to live in. The emphasis must be clearly focused on the needs of the individual resident. The older person should not have to fit into established systems, frameworks and practices. This may require the owners and staff to reassess traditional roles, routines, duties and the environmental atmosphere, to create a greater flexibility. Drawing on experienced people to translate the NOS will help, e.g. health visitors. According to the UKCC (1997), Health visitors have specialist knowledge and skills in the promotion and maintenance of health of the older person, and could assist the team in addressing ethical and moral dilemmas. The residential team also need to make contact with the local 'community' to involve them in all community and health promotion programmes from voluntary and statutory services, so that the philosophy of the 'home' is seen by professionals and lay people as that of any other 'home' in the community. The philosophy of the home needs to be a two-way process, where residents take part in community activities outside the home and local health promotion initiatives are brought into it. Local health promotion departments have health promotion advisors responsible for promoting the health of older people in the community, and they too could act as facilitators. Tools such as the Royal College of Nursing (RCN 1997) Assessment Tool for Nursing Older People can also help. It is intended to be used as part of the overall assessment of a resident in a care home. It incorporates physical, biological, psychosocial, psychological and functional aspects of the older person's life. The tool describes a holistic framework which includes these functions:

- supportive;
- restorative;

- educative;
- life-enhancing;
- managerial.

They are seen as the main roles of nursing activities 'on behalf of' and 'with' the residents and staff. They need to be addressed in the context of a team approach. The main issue that we must not forget when addressing the maintenance and promotion of health (whether we are using NOS, the RCN tool or any other tools) is how we communicate with the residents. According to Lanceley (1985) language can be controlling, and instead of leading to the empowerment of the residents, techniques we use to communicate, such as our choice of words, can lead to a sense of helpless dependence rather than confident autonomy.

In this chapter I have explored the concept of health promotion in residential settings. Older people have complex individual needs, but theoretical frameworks emphasize key issues enabling us to envisage possibilities for practice. Older people have a responsibility to maintain and promote their own health, but their health cannot be divorced from the social and economic environment in which they live. The residential setting must be conducive to the empowerment of both the residents and the staff. The health of older people is related to the concept of control and associated positive self image. As Tones (1993) suggests, environmental adaptation and education designed to enhance control not only results in a better quality of life for older people but also improves their life expectancy.

References

Allen, I., Hogg, D., Peace, S. (1992) *Elderly People: Choice, Participation and Satisfaction*. London: Policy Studies Institute.

Care Sector Consortium (1997) *National Occupational Standards. Professional Activity in Health Promotion and Care: Introductory Guide*. London: Local Government Management Board.

Counsel and Care (1992) *From Home to a Home*. London: Counsel and Care.

Doyal, L. and Gough, I. (1991) *A Theory of Human Need*. Basingstoke: Macmillan Press.

Ebrahim, S. and Davey Smith, G. (1996) *Health Promotion in Older People for the Prevention of Coronary Heart Disease and Stroke*. London: HEA.

Ewles, L. and Simnett, I. (1999) *Promoting Health: A Practical Guide*. London: Baillière Tindall and RCN.

Lanceley, A. (1985) Use of controlling language in the rehabilitation of the elderly, *Journal of Advanced Nursing*, 10: 125–35.

Langer, E. J. and Rodin, J. (1976), The effects of enhanced personal responsibility for the aged, *Journal of Personality and Social Psychology*, 34: 191–8.

Naidoo, J. and Wills, J. (1995) *Health Promotion: Foundations for Practice*. London: Baillière Tindall, W. B. Saunders.

Naidoo, J. and Wills, J. (1998) *Practising Health Promotion: Dilemma and Challenges*. London: Baillière Tindall, W. B. Saunders, RCN.

Nolan, M. and Caldock, K. (1996) Assessment: identifying the barriers to good practice, *Health and Social Care in the Community*, 4(2): 77–85.

Nolan, M., Grant, G. and Keady, J. (1996) *Understanding Family Care*. Buckingham: Open University Press.

Prochaska, J. O. and DiClemente, C. (1984) *The Transtheoretical Approach: Crossing Traditional Foundations of Change*. Homewood, IL: Don Jones/Irwin.

Rambo, B. J. (1984) *Adaptation Nursing: Assessment and Intervention*. Philadelphia: W. B. Saunders.

Royal College of Nursing (1997) *Assessment Tool for Nursing Older People*, London: RCN.

Schober, J. (1989) Approaches to nursing care, in S. M. Hinchliff, S. E. Norman, and J. Schober (eds) *Nursing Practice and Health Care*. London: Edward Arnold.

Secretary of State for Health (1992) *The Health of the Nation: A Strategy for Health in England*. London: HMSO.

Sinclair, I. (1998) The elderly, in I. Sinclair (ed.) *Residential Care: The Research Reviewed*. London: Stationery Office.

Tones, K. (1993) The theory of health promotion: implications for nursing, in J. Wilson-Barnett and J. Macleod Clark (eds) *Research in Health Promotion and Nursing*. London: Macmillan Press.

Tones, K. and Tilford, S. (1994) *Health Education: Effectiveness, Efficiency and Equity*, 2nd edn. London: Chapman & Hall.

Tones, K., Tilford, S. and Robinson, Y. (1991) *Health Education: Effectiveness and Efficiency*. London: Chapman & Hall.

UKCC (United Kingdom Central Council) (1997) *The Continuing Care of Older People. The UKCC Policy Paper*. London: UKCC.

United Nations European Resource Unit UK (1999) The International Year of Older Persons, *Ageing and Health: A Global Challenge for the 21st Century*. Presentations at the WHO symposium held at Kobe Centre, Japan, 10–13 November 1998. Kobe, Japan: WHO Centre.

Victor, C. V. (1995) *Health and Health Care in Later Life*. Buckingham: Open University Press.

Wallace, R. (1994) Assessing the health of individuals and population in surveys of the elderly: some concepts and approaches, *The Gerontologist*, 14(4): 449–53.

Weinstein, N. (1994) Why it won't happen to me: perceptions of risk factors and illness susceptibility, *Health Psychology*, 3: 431–57.

World Health Organization (WHO) (1993) *European Health Promotion Policy*. Copenhagen: WHO Regional Office for Europe.

___11___

Health and the older traveller: issues for health promotion

STEPHEN CLIFT AND MATTHEW MORRISSEY

> Are you planning the holiday of a lifetime or hoping to visit family or friends? If so, and you are either older or have a disability, don't be put off travelling by air because you fear that any difficulties you have may be insuperable. With a little knowledge and forethought, practically anyone can travel by air.
>
> (Disabled Living Foundation 1994: 4)

> There is often an assumption that advancing years alone rob the individual of physical and mental prowess and steal away independence. Compensatory mechanisms, the accrued wisdom of years and sound medical advice can, however, ensure that most global holidaymakers will travel in good health.
>
> (McIntosh 1992: 2)

Introduction

It will be obvious to anyone passing through a major international airport that international travellers span the entire age range, from newborn babies to the older and infirm approaching the end of their life span. Globally since the Second World War, and certainly in affluent industrialized countries, life expectancy has increased significantly, and populations in Western countries have become progressively older. These trends are set to continue into the near future. Recent projections for the UK, for example, show that the relative proportions of teenagers and retired people in the British population will soon reverse, and that by 2021 there will be substantially more people living in retirement than those in their teenage years (Woodward 1999). An increasing proportion of retired people also have the financial wherewithal, and the time, to travel. For 15 or more years post-retirement, if they remain fit and free from health problems which render travel inadvisable or impossible, many older people take advantage of their new-found freedom from work and other responsibilities to travel widely.

When older people travel abroad, what health risks might they face, and what should health professionals and older travellers themselves do to ensure that these risks are kept to a minimum? In answering these questions, this chapter begins by presenting a general perspective on international travel and health as a context for focusing on the potential health risks faced by young old and old old people when they travel internationally. Little empirical research has focused specifically on older travellers, but some findings from research on travel and health which has surveyed a wide age range of tourists are reviewed. Finally, the central role of primary health care professionals in ensuring that older people are well informed and prepared prior to travel is highlighted.

The health dimensions of international travel

The last quarter of the twentieth century saw dramatic increases in the scale of international tourism (World Tourism Organization 1998). Not only has the volume of tourism increased but so too has the average distance travelled as tourists from the more affluent, Westernized countries increasingly visit destinations outside their own region – especially in poorer Third World countries. Commercial tourism products have also diversified, and the international tourist has on offer a tremendous variety of options available in addition to the traditional organized package in one resort: guided tours with a historical/cultural focus; sea cruises from Alaska to the Antarctic; holidays involving challenging activities and sports; independent trekking in remoter regions; holidays for self development and spiritual exploration; and trips to destinations which offer easy opportunities for sex – commercial or otherwise – in destinations throughout the world.

Since mid-twentieth century, the World Tourism Organisation has gathered statistics on international arrivals, which show how dramatic the growth of international travel and tourism has been, from just over 25 million arrivals in 1950 to over 600 million in 1997 – a 24-fold increase (Hundt 1996; World Tourism Organization 1998).

The health implications of mass leisure tourism attracted scant research attention until the late 1970s and early 1980s (Cook 1995; Hellen 1995). At that time a number of factors led to concern about the health risks tourists might be exposed to, in travelling long distances and holidaying in tropical regions:

- the growth of long-haul travel and the increased scale of travel;
- the development of tourism industries in Third World countries;
- the re-emergence of diseases thought to be under control or declining (e.g. malaria);
- the appearance of new diseases never seen before (e.g. HIV/AIDS);
- increasing levels of drug and antibiotic resistance among infectious organisms.

In response to such concerns the late 1980s saw the establishment of the first WHO collaborating centre on tourist health in Rimini, and the first international conferences on travel and health, which led to the formation of the

International Society for Travel Medicine (ISTM) in 1991. Since 1993, ISTM has published the *Journal of Travel Medicine*. Interest in the health dimensions of tourism has also developed recently among academics in social science, health promotion and tourism studies (Clift and Page 1996; Clift and Grabowski 1997; Clift and Carter 1999).

Since its establishment in 1948, the World Health Organization has played a key role in monitoring global health patterns and in providing guidance on travel and health issues. Each year it publishes the book *International Travel and Health: Vaccination Requirements and Health Advice*. This publication provides information on yellow fever vaccination requirements, the malaria situation worldwide and the 'geographical distribution of potential health hazards to travellers'. Finally guidance is given to travellers on a variety of potential risks to health during travel and how they can be avoided. These include: hazards associated with environmental factors; risks from food and drink; sexually transmitted infections, including HIV; a range of infectious diseases, including malaria, dengue and tuberculosis and vaccinations. As an indication of the nature and scale of health problems associated with international travel, Table 11.1 reports the estimated incidence of the most common health problems arising among travellers from Europe and the United States visiting developing countries.

Travellers' diarrhoea is clearly the most commonly reported health problem, with between 30 and 80 per cent of travellers affected. Malaria ranks second, with 2.5 per cent of travellers to West African destinations who do not take chemo-prophylaxis affected by this problem. (The estimate given is not the proportion of all visitors to malarial regions who contract malaria, since a substantial proportion will take adequate precautions. Assuming that approximately 10 per cent of visitors fail to take adequate precautions, a better estimate of incidence among all travellers would be 0.25 per cent.) In the case of gonorrhoea, 0.2 per cent of travellers are said to return with this infection, and for HIV the figure is 0.01 per cent. The figure for all forms of sexually transmitted infections is of course likely to be greater. It should also be noted that the issue of risks of sexually transmitted infections in the context of travel

Table 11.1   Health problems among travellers from Europe and North America to developing countries

Health problems	Percentage incidence	Numbers per 100,000
Travellers' diarrhoea	30–80	30,000–80,000
Malaria (West Africa, no chemo-prophylaxis	2.5	2,500
Respiratory tract infection	1.5	1,500
Hepatitis A	0.3	300
Gonorrhoea	0.2	200
HIV infection	0.01	10

Source: World Health Organization (1999).

is not confined to 'developing countries' to the same degree as travellers' diarrhoea and malaria. Travellers who are sexually active with new partners, and who do not take adequate precautions, run some risk of sexually transmitted infections whatever their destination.

The general picture provided by the WHO regarding travel and health risks represents a compilation of findings from a wide range of surveillance and research studies on travel and health, and provides no details of factors, such as age, which might be associated with higher or lower incidence of health risks. Age is commonly a factor considered in specific studies of travel and health, but, to date, very little research attention has been focused on the circumstances, experiences, health problems and health needs of older travellers. The next section of this chapter summarizes some of the key issues identified by medical practitioners with a particular interest in the health of older travellers, and reviews some of the evidence on age differences in relation to travel and health.

Older travellers and health

In the most important contribution to the literature on older people and travel, McIntosh (1992: 2) provides a valuable and succinct general assessment of the significance of ageing in respect of travel and health. Older travellers, he suggests, fall into three categories in terms of their health risks while travelling:

1 The low-risk group. The 'young' old; those journeying to low risk destinations; those on short-haul journeys; those free from any predisposing illness.
2 The medium-risk group. Includes group 1 where travel involves environmental extremes or tropical countries; the frail old; those with pre-existing illness.
3 The high-risk group. The medically unfit; the terminally ill; those on last-fling holidays; those with pre-existing illness travelling to high-risk venues; those presenting with pre-existing illness to areas of environmental extremes and to tropical countries.

With respect to the first category, there is clearly little reason to believe that young old or old old people travelling from, say, Norway for a two-week holiday in the south of France will face any greater risks or problems with their health than they would at home. Health and safety standards in transportation, hotel accommodation, water quality, sanitation and food handling are high across the whole of Europe, and assuming that patterns of activity and leisure behaviour in which older travellers engage are no riskier on holiday than at home, a holiday is more likely to be beneficial to general well-being and health than it is to present increased hazards.

Nevertheless, it is clearly the case that ageing does bring with it a general decline in physical strength and a reduction in the efficiency of many bodily functions. If travel involves any substantial increase in the demands placed on different systems of the body, then older travellers, especially old old and those with pre-existing illness, in general, will be less able to cope with such stresses, and may be at greater risk of health problems. McIntosh (1992: 3) provides a useful summary of the changes in bodily functions associated with ageing which have relevance to global travel, especially where travel:

- is long, arduous and entails restricted mobility (e.g. long-haul air travel);
- involves environmental extremes (e.g. of temperature, altitude or humidity);
- entails potential exposure to exotic infections (e.g. in travel to tropical destinations).

Some of the major effects of ageing of relevance to travel and health are given in Table 11.2.

Table 11.2 Effects of the ageing process likely to have an impact on health risks in the context of global travel

Changes occur in	Effects
Water, sodium and temperature regulation	Decreased sodium and water conservation, decreased sweating ability, increased risks of hyperthermia, dehydration and heat exhaustion in hot climates.
Cardiopulmonary function	Decrease in pulmonary function, decrease in ventilatory response to hypoxia, increased cardiac load. Risks associated with low partial pressure in an aircraft or at altitude, and enforced immobility during long-haul flights (venous thrombosis and pulmonary embolism).
Gastrointestinal function	Increased achlordydria, decreased ability to cope with infection. Greater risk of diarrhoeal diseases.
Cell-mediated immune response	Decreased ability to fight off infection. Increased risk of exotic illness in travel to tropical destinations.
Neurological function	Decreased ability to acquire, retain and retrieve information. Greater potential for confusion in the context of busy international airports and during travel, coping with cultural differences and communication problems.
Metabolic response	Decrease in glucose tolerance response to physiological stress. Greater difficulty in coping with the physical demands of travel, turbulence and circadian rhythm changes.

Source: McIntosh (1992, 1998).

Research findings on age and travel health problems

Research evidence certainly supports McIntosh's contention that older travellers may, in general, be at lower risk of certain travel-related health problems than younger travellers. One of the earliest substantial studies of travel and health began in Glasgow in the early 1970s when the then Communicable Diseases (Scotland) Unit established a surveillance system to monitor the health experience of the general population of returning Scottish travellers, and also to focus on specific groups of travellers following an alert about a possible health problem (Cossar 1993). Over a period of 15 years, data were gathered from a total of 14,227 respondents following arrival at Glasgow airport from points of departure mainly in Europe and North Africa. A majority of travellers experienced no health problems at all during travel, but no fewer than 37 per cent of returning tourists reported some illness – predominantly diarrhoea, vomiting and other alimentary symptoms, which affected 76 per cent of all those who reported illness. Interestingly, however, reports of illness declined with increasing age. The highest attack rates were found among the under-40 age group, with 41 per cent of 10–19-year-olds and 48 per cent of 20–29-year-olds reporting illness, compared with 28 per cent of those aged 50–59 years, and only 20 per cent among those aged 60 and above.

Studies conducted elsewhere on the health experiences of tourists have reported similar results. Steffen *et al.* (1983), in a study of travellers' diarrhoea among 16,568 randomly selected Swiss tourists, found an attack rate of 28 per cent, with the age group most affected being 20–29-year-olds. More recently, Steffen *et al.* (1999) undertook a major study of travellers' diarrhoea among short-term visitors to Jamaica. Over 30,000 respondents participated by completing a questionnaire just prior to returning home. The overall attack rate for travellers' diarrhoea was 23.6 per cent, with 11.7 per cent reporting severe diarrhoea and the rest suffering moderate or mild symptoms. Attack rates significantly declined with age, with 26.3 per cent of 16–35-year-olds and 20.2 per cent of 35–55-year-olds affected, but only 12.1 per cent of those over the age of 55 reporting symptoms. Steffen *et al.* (1999) note that the medical impact of travellers' diarrhoea is considerable and that tourists with a severe attack were incapacitated for an average of just over 17 hours.

Page *et al.* (1994) report a more wide-ranging survey of tourist health issues in which 785 British tourists on holiday in Malta were asked about travel advice prior to travel, health precautions, holiday behaviours which might carry health risks and health problems experienced. Malta attracts large numbers of British tourists each year and is particularly popular with older, retired visitors. It is also undoubtedly a safe destination for tourists. Nevertheless, a number of strong age trends emerged from this study which raise interesting issues regarding the experiences of older travellers:

- with increasing age tourists were less likely to have taken sun creams on holiday;
- with increasing age tourists were more likely to have prescribed medicines with them;
- older tourists were more cautious with their diet on holiday, preferring to

eat in hotels and avoiding food from street vendors, taking ice in their drinks and eating ice cream;
- with increasing age tourists were less likely to swim in the sea or in swimming pools;
- older tourists were somewhat less likely to drink alcohol on holiday and were markedly less likely to report increased consumption compared with home than younger tourists;
- headache was the most common health problem reported, and this showed a strong age trend, with respondents in their teens and twenties reporting headaches at over twice the rate of those in the oldest age category;
- sunburn also showed a clear age trend, with visitors in their teens and twenties more than twice as likely to have experienced sunburn as those aged 60 plus (despite being more likely to have taken sun cream).

In a further study of tourist health in Malta, Clark and Clift (1996) gathered data from 413 tourists, in their teens through to their seventies, on health problems and aspects of their holiday experiences. Just over 13 per cent of tourists reported some health problem during their holiday, with 5.2 per cent reporting diarrhoea, vomiting or upset stomach and 3.1 per cent reporting sunburn/sunstroke. Health problems were uncommon and minor. Of much greater interest, however, were tourists' responses on a 28-item questionnaire designed to assess aspects of their holiday behaviour and experiences, many of which have implications for health (either positively or negatively).

Substantial and significant age differences emerged for no fewer than 16 of these items, with half of these showing higher endorsement by the teens to thirties age group (e.g. 'tried to build up a suntan', 'had a romantic relationship' and 'drank more alcohol'), some being more endorsed by the middle-aged group of those in their forties and fifties (e.g. 'taken more exercise than at home', 'relaxed more than at home') and some more frequently endorsed by the oldest age group in their sixties and seventies (e.g. 'careful to avoid sunburn', 'careful to avoid infections', 'reflected on the meaning of life'). Factor analysis of the responses to these items identified three clearly interpretable dimensions, which were labelled 'sun, sex and sangria', 'enjoyment versus stress' and 'personal growth and activity'. Younger tourists, and especially those on holiday without a partner, gained the highest scores on the first factor, and older tourists scored significantly more highly on the third.

It would appear, therefore, that older tourists on holiday in Malta are more conscious of health risks, less likely to engage in activities which might carry such risks and more reflective and inward-looking.

General age trends such as these disguise the fact, however, that considerable variations occurred in each age group and that other factors, such as holiday companions, were also important influences on holiday behaviour and experience. This was particularly clear with respect to three items relating to social life and relationships on holiday. Table 11.3 reports the percentage levels of agreement with statements about nightlife, flirting and romantic relationships on holiday. The results show that endorsement was invariably higher among the youngest group, especially among those on holiday without

Table 11.3   Aspects of the holiday experiences of British tourists in Malta

	On holiday without a partner			On holiday with a partner		
Holiday experience	*Teens to 30s (n = 76)*	*40s to 50s (n = 33)*	*60s to 70s (n = 27)*	*Teens to 30s (n = 70)*	*40s to 50s (n = 93)*	*60s to 70s (n = 111)*
Exciting night life (%)	57	18	26	34	22	22
Enjoyed flirting (%)	61	30	36	23	17	19
Romantic relationship (%)	25	3	13	3	1	4

a partner, but substantial minorities of the older age group on holiday without a partner reported flirting and getting involved in romantic relationships. The figures for those on holiday without a partner are especially interesting: a quarter of those in their teens to late thirties report a romantic involvement, which falls to only 3 per cent among those in their forties and fifties and rises again to 12.5 per cent among those in their sixties and seventies. While respondents were not questioned specifically about sex on holiday, these findings do suggest that some older tourists may be sexually active with new partners on holiday. The sexual life of older people continues to be an under-researched area, and almost all studies of sexual health risks in the context of travel have tended to focus exclusively on younger travellers (Mulhall 1996; Elliott *et al.* 1998; Bloor and Thomas 1999). As McIntosh (1992: 94) points out, however,

> The risk of HIV infection is now a global problem and older travellers, like the young, should avoid sexual contact where there is a risk of infection. Age is not a barrier to sexually acquired disease and 2.6% of men admitted to a sexual relationship with a prostitute while abroad in a recent study of older people attending a genito-urinary clinic in the UK.

As noted above, concerns about health in the context of travel arise primarily in relation to tourists from affluent, industrialized countries travelling to less developed, often tropical countries, where health, safety and hygiene standards may be lower and risks of communicable diseases higher. If Malta can be considered a safe destination, The Gambia, by comparison, poses enhanced risks, especially of malaria, and such risks have been the focus of recent studies by Clift *et al.* (1997) and Abraham *et al.* (1999). In the earlier study a sample of 113 British tourists aged from their teens to their seventies were interviewed while on holiday in The Gambia and questioned about health precautions, malaria prophylaxis and health problems, and 78 were followed up after their return home. A majority of tourists experienced no health problems at all while on holiday, and only small minorities reported more than mild symptoms (e.g. 19.5 per cent reported diarrhoea, with only 3.5 per cent describing the diarrhoea as severe). In addition, however, over a third of tourists reported being bitten by insects, and 5.3 per cent rated the bites as severe.

At the time of this study, considerable controversy had arisen over potential side-effects associated with the use of the anti-malarial drug mefloquine.

Just prior to the study, the BBC consumer affairs programme, *Watchdog*, ran features highlighting the risk of severe side-effects associated with the use of mefloquine – in particular its role in precipitating psychiatric problems. It was clear during the fieldwork in The Gambia that most tourists were aware of this controversy, having seen the programme itself, or been informed of its contents by friends or relatives. Where tourists had been concerned about potential side-effects before travelling, they generally sought further information or reassurance by consulting their GP or practice nurse or a pharmacist. Out of the sample interviewed, four people were not taking malaria prophylaxis, and of those who were, three-quarters were taking mefloquine. Just over a quarter of tourists taking malaria prophylaxis reported 'problems' which they attributed to the tablets.

Tourist age had little bearing on reported health precautions, health problems or side-effects while on holiday, but during the follow-up interviews an issue of substantially greater concern to older tourists emerged very graphically. In all the following extracts from interviews with older women, concerns are voiced regarding the advisability of their husbands taking mefloquine given that they were on medication for existing health problems.

> Well, actually what happened was, we got the prescription from the GP for Lariam tablets (mefloquine). I hadn't actually got them but I saw the programme on TV and we hadn't had these tablets before – because my husband has arthritis bad and he's on nineteen tablets a day – what was it going to do to him? So I went to see the doctor and asked him about them . . .

> We asked the pharmacist that we got them from and we asked – you know – what reactions we would get because my husband is on medication so we check on all tablets to see if they'll react with them. So she gave us what everyone else had been told, so we asked about all the publicity they'd had and she said 'Well, you know, it's up to you, one in so many thousand chances, so which would you rather have?' and we took the chance.

> Lariam was advised by the practice nurse. We were given a private prescription for that and I was told by two people quite passionately that I must not take them and George must not take them. Really adamant. So what I did, because my husband suffers from high blood pressure, I went down and said was that compatible for the thing with the blood pressure? They said, 'Oh yes, that's all right,' so then I went and saw my pharmacist who also assured me it was okay to take the Lariam.

(Clift *et al.* 1997: 112–13)

These quotations illustrate very clearly the circumstances of young old and old old travellers falling in categories 2 and 3 identified by McIntosh (1992). Where existing health problems raise concerns for intending older travellers, they should clearly consult their own doctor or a specialist in travel medicine.

Health promotion and the older traveller

Both quotations cited at the beginning of this chapter highlight the importance of information and preparation for ensuring healthy travel. This is generally true for travellers of all ages, especially when travelling to destinations which pose increased risks to health, and is all the more true for older travellers falling in categories 2 and 3 identified by McIntosh (1992). In the UK, travel health advice is available from many sources:

- the Department of Health publishes general health advice for travellers;
- travel health campaigns have been run both nationally and locally in recent years (see Stears 1996);
- tour companies offer advice to their customers in brochures and pre-travel literature;
- commercial companies publish holiday health guides (e.g. Boots);
- most travel guides to specific destinations include information on health risks (e.g. Lonely Planet guides);
- specialist travel health guides are available;
- travel health information can be gained from specialist telephone help lines (e.g. Medical Advice Service for Travellers Abroad, MASTA) and through the Internet.

Travel health information in such sources is generally given without reference to the age of travellers, however, and rarely addresses the particular health needs of older travellers. The otherwise excellent guide to healthy travel recently published by Haines and Thorowgood (1998), for instance, has no section addressing the health needs of older travellers, and even those sections which could readily highlight the enhanced risks faced by the older fail to do so. In a section on health and air travel, for instance, the following passage appears:

> The decompression and forced inactivity [during long distance flights] can also cause the swelling of limbs and feet which sometimes prevents travellers wearing their normal shoes for up to 24 hours on arrival. This is dangerous because swollen legs can cause blood clots which, when they break free, can lodge in the lungs and cause a pulmonary embolism. A 1988 report in the *Lancet* estimated that over three years at Heathrow Airport, 18 per cent of the 61 sudden deaths in long distance passengers were caused by clots on the lungs, a figure far higher than the incidence in the general population.

> (Haines and Thorowgood 1998)

Recent research has established that long-distance travel with restricted mobility is certainly connected with venous thromboembolic disease (deep venous thrombosis and pulmonary embolism) among people over the age of 60 (Ferrari *et al.* 1999). It is clear, therefore, that information on travel and health should be qualified with respect to the age of travellers. Embolisms (e.g. pulmonary) are a real consideration on long-haul flights, especially for older travellers.

The most appropriate source of advice for older travellers is undoubtedly their general practitioner, or more often a practice nurse running a travel health clinic within a primary health care setting. Primary health care professionals have access to an individual's medical history and are in a position to offer detailed advice given that history and the details of the traveller's planned itinerary. They are reliant, however, on epidemiological surveillance information on the nature of travel-related health risks and developments in health protection in the travel field. While a range of publications provide up-to-date information, and professionals increasingly have access to travel health software and call upon specialist services provided by pharmaceutical companies, it is still the case that many primary health care professionals offering travel health advice, especially family doctors, have not received specialist training in travel health (Carroll *et al.* 1998). A large majority of primary health professionals surveyed by Carroll *et al.* were interested in receiving training in the area of travel health, however, and the particular needs of older travellers would clearly be an appropriate issue for any training course to address. Such training could draw on the many graphic case histories provided by McIntosh (1992) of health difficulties experienced by individuals in their seventies and above in the context of travel.

Conclusion

It should be stressed that international travel, for the vast majority of travellers, is remarkably safe and free from health problems – especially if they are well informed and well prepared. This is also true for older and old old travellers. It is safe, because time and energy and money are invested in maintaining standards and in protecting and promoting health, and because, by and large, most people are careful not to expose themselves to obvious risks. Of course, if older travellers have existing medical conditions, there will be a greater need to plan international travel with care, and to seek appropriate medical advice. As the older population of Western societies continues to grow, and assumes a greater proportion of the total population, so the number of older travellers will increase, with an increasing need for primary health care professionals to provide support and sound practical advice to help people to realize their remaining dreams of travel.

References

Abraham, C., Clift, S. and Grabowski, P. (1999) Cognitive predictors of adherence to malaria prophylaxis regimens on return from a malarious region: a prospective studies, *Social Science and Medicine*, 48, 1641–54.

Bloor, M. and Thomas, M. (1999) Sexual risk behaviour in a sample of 5676 young, unaccompanied travellers, in S. Clift and S. Carter (eds) *Tourism and Sex: Culture, Commerce and Coercion*. London: Pinter.

Bradley, D. J., Warhurst, D. C., Blaze, M., Smith, V. and Williams, J. (1998) Malaria imported into the United Kingdom in 1996, *Eurosurveillance*, 3(4): 40–2.

Carroll, B., Behrens, R. H. and Crichton, D. (1998) Primary health care needs for travel medicine training in Britain, *Journal of Travel Medicine*, 5(1): 3–6.

Cartwright, R. Y. and Chahed, M. (1997) Foodborne diseases in travellers, *World Health Statistical Quarterly*, 50: 102–10.

Clark, N. and Clift, S. (1996) Dimensions of holiday experiences and their health implications: a study of British tourists in Malta, in S. Clift and S. Page (eds) *Health and the International Tourist*. London: Routledge.

Clift, S. and Carter, S. (1999) *Tourism and Sex: Culture, Commerce and Coercion*. London: Cassell.

Clift, S. and Grabowski, P. (1997) *Tourism and Health: Risks, Research and Responses*. London: Pinter.

Clift, S., Grabowski, P. and Sharpley, R. (1997) British tourists in The Gambia: health precautions and malaria prophylaxis, in S. Clift and P. Grabowski (eds) *Tourism and Health: Risks, Research and Responses*. London: Pinter.

Clift, S. and Page, S. (eds) (1996) *Health and the International Tourist*. London: Routledge.

Cook, G. C. (ed.)(1995) *Travel-associated Disease*. London: Royal College of Physicians of London.

Cossar, J. H. (1993) Travellers' health – a review, *Travel Medicine International*, February: 17–26.

Disabled Living Foundation (1994) *Flying High: A Practical Guide to Air Travel for Older People and People with Disabilities*. London: Disabled Living Foundation.

Elliott, L., Morrison, A., Ditton, J. *et al.* (1998) Alcohol, drug use, and sexual behaviour of young adults on a Mediterranean dance holiday, *Addiction Research*, 5(4): 1–22.

Ferrari, E., Chevallier, T., Chapelier, A. and Baudouy, M. (1999) Travel as a risk factor for venous thromboembolic disease, *Chest*, 115(2): 440–4.

Haines, M. and Thorowgood, S. (1998) *The Traveller's Healthbook*. London: WEXAS International.

Hellen, J. A. (1995) Tourist health and tourist medicine in the tropics: a case for sustainable development?, in B. F. Iyun, Y. Verhasselt and J. A. Hellen (eds) *The Health of Nations: Medicine, Disease and Development in the Third World*. Aldershot: Avebury.

Hundt, A. (1996) Impact of tourism development on the economy and health of Third World nations, *Journal of Travel Medicine*, 3(2): 107–12.

McIntosh, I. B. (1992) *Travel and Health in the Older: A Medical Handbook*. London: Quay Publishing.

McIntosh, I. B. (1998) Health hazards and the older traveller, *Journal of Travel Medicine*, 5(1): 27–9.

Mulhall, B. P. (1996) Sex and travel: studies of sexual behaviour, disease and health promotion in international travellers – a global review, *International Journal of STD & AIDS*, 7: 455–65.

Page, S. J., Clift, S. and Clark, N. (1994) Tourist health: the precautions, behaviour and health problems of British tourists in Malta, in A. V. Seaton *et al.* (eds) *Tourism: The State of the Art*. London: Wiley.

Stears, D. F. (1996) Travel health promotion, in S. Clift and S. Page (eds) *Health and the International Tourist*. London: Routledge.

Steffen, R., Collard, F., Tornieporth, N. *et al.* (1999) Epidemiology, etiology, and impact of travelers' diarrhea in Jamaica, *Journal of the American Medical Association*, 281(9): 811–17.

Steffen, R., van der Linde, F., Syr, K. and Schar, M. (1983) Epidemiology of diarrhoea in travellers, *Journal of the American Medical Association*, 248: 1176–80.

Woodward, W. (1999) Greying of Britain will put children in the shade, *Guardian*, 29 May: 3.

World Health Organization (1999) *International Travel and Health: Vaccination Requirements and Health Advice*. Geneva: World Health Organization

World Tourism Organization (1998) *Tourism Highlights 1997*. Madrid: World Tourism Organization.

Index

Note: page numbers in italics refer to figures or tables.

PROMOTING HEALTH IN OLD AGE
CRITICAL ISSUES IN SELF HEALTH CARE

Miriam Bernard

During the last quarter of the twentieth century, there has been a growing interest in health issues and older people. Although older people make considerable
use of health and welfare services, researchers, practitioners and policy makers
often forget that the majority of them live active and healthy lifestyles, taking
care of themselves with a minimum of formal support. Self-care is therefore
crucial to the maintenance of well-being yet it has often been neglected when
considering later life.

This book explores the theory, extent and practice of self health care in later life.
It brings together literature from the areas of health education and promotion,
self-help and self-care, and gerontology, in order to provide an overview of the
main research approaches and developments in this field. It critically examines
the self health care practices and capacities of older people, using illustrative
results from an ongoing innovative action research project.

Promtoing Health in Old Age is aimed at students taking courses on gerontology,
nursing, medicine, social work, social sciences and women's studies. It will also
be of interest to practitioners in the field and those involved in the planning
and delivery of services to older adults.

Contents
*The challenge of an ageing population – Promoting health in old age – Perspectives on
self health care – Developments in self health care – Self health care in practice: the self
health care in old age project – Research in action: evaluating the self health care in old
age project – Self health care in action: participation, accessibility and informed choice
among older people – Self health care in action: skills development and empowerment
among older people – Self health care in action: its impact on volunteers and staff – Learning the lessons: the role of self health care in future policy and practice – References –
Index.*

208pp   0 335 19247 5 (Paperback)   0 335 19248 3 (Hardback)

STORIES OF AGEING

Mike Hepworth

- How is ageing represented in popular fiction?
- What is the role of the imagination in making sense of growing older?
- Do the ideas and images in popular fiction correspond or relate to ideas and images of ageing found in social gerontology?

This innovative book reflects the growing interest within gerontology in fictional representations of older age. It is about stories of ageing – full-length novels with central characters who are in the later part of life (50+) and experiencing the process of ageing as they move into older age. The book draws on symbolic interactionism for its main themes and centres around popular fiction that is widely read and easily available. Ranging from Agatha Christie through to Penelope Lively and Joanna Trollope, it shows how the novel can be a useful source of information about ways we all make sense of growing old. It looks at characters' personal experience of ageing, and the tensions between this and social attitudes towards them. These interactions are very difficult to research using conventional techniques of social investigation and readers are encouraged to explore their own selection of novels for other examples of meanings attached to the ageing process.

Stories of Ageing is engaging and accessible in ways rarely evident in existing literary gerontology. The aim is to enthuse readers to compare their own interpretations of the stories with stories of others, and thus to relate fictions of ageing to their own experience and to the work of social gerontologists. As a book combining sociological analysis, literature and a gerontological agenda, it is the first in its field. It opens up fiction as a resource for anyone interested in the process of growing old and is essential reading for all students, researchers and practitioners in the field.

Contents
Introduction – Stories of ageing – Body and self – Self and others – Objects, places and spaces – Vulnerability and risk – Futures – References – Index.

160pp   0 335 19853 8 (Paperback)   0 335 19854 6 (Hardback)

HEALTH IN OLD AGE
MYTH, MYSTERY AND MANAGEMENT

Moyra Sidell

- Why do many older people rate their health as good when 'objective' evidence suggests that old age is a time of inevitable decline and disease?
- How do different perspectives on health inform our understanding of health in old age?
- What are the policy implications for ensuring a healthy future for old age?

This book addresses important questions which existing literature on health and old age has largely ignored. By juxtaposing detailed case histories and first person accounts from older people with 'official statistics' on the health of 'the elderly' it explores the myths and tries to unpick the mysteries which surround the subject of health in later life. It goes on to explore the implications of these myths and mysteries for the way individual older people manage their health. It looks at the resources and social support available to them as well as the implications for public policy provision. The book ends by exploring the problems and possibilities of ensuring a healthy future for old age. It will be essential reading for reflective practitioners and for anyone concerned with new developments in the fields of ageing, social policy and health.

Contents
Introduction – Part 1: The health context – The mirage of health – Lay logic – Patterns of health and illness among older people – Part 2: Experiencing health – Understanding chronic illness and disability – Maintaining health with physical illness and functional disability – Maintaining health with mental malaise – Part 3: Resources for health – Health care and the management of health – Personal resources and social support – A healthy future for old age – Bibliography – Index.

200pp   0 335 19136 3 (Paperback)   0 335 19336 6 (Hardback)